The Spirit's Tether

The Spirit's Tether

Sermons For Pentecost
(First Third)
Cycle B Gospel Texts

Leonard H. Budd

CSS Publishing Company, Inc.
Lima, Ohio

THE SPIRIT'S TETHER

Library of Congress Cataloging-in-Publication Data

Budd, Leonard H., 1933-
    The Spirit's tether : sermons for Pentecost (first third) gospel, cycle B / by Leonard H. Budd.
        p.   cm.
    ISBN 1-55673-608-8
    1. Pentecost season — Sermons. 2. Sermons, American. 3. Bible. N.T. Gospels — Sermons. I. Title.
    BV61.B84   1993
252'.6—dc20   93-2757
                                                                        CIP

9333 / ISBN 1-55673-608-8   PRINTED IN U.S.A.

Create in me a clean heart,
O God,
And put a new and right
spirit within me.

— Psalm 51:10

Table Of Contents

C - Common; L - Lutheran; RC - Roman Catholic

Introduction

As the sun broke over the edge of the city wall it brought warmth back to the little doorways where old men sat. The sun's heat, in its first brush after the cold night, made steam rise from the flat, stone surfaces. Jerusalem, set upon the high mountain, captured the cold of night so that windows were shuttered and the heaviest cloaks were wrapped tight. But with a new day's sun upon the stone, the city warmed. Windows opened. Doors were tethered open. Humanity moved outside to begin the business of another day.

Only this day the sun announced the Pentecost holiday. Visitors from distant lands now filled the streets. They crowded the marketplaces, bartering for food. Wise merchants knew the coin of every realm. They were not outbid by foreign traders. On this Pentecost the market square was filled. Even the doorways were crowded and the din of human voices was matched by the braying of animals, the barking of dogs, the scraping of heavy boxes upon the worn stone walks.

The entrance to the square held the well. It provided the only water for that part of Jerusalem. A young man stood by the wood frame staring long and hard upon the crowds. It appeared from his dress that he was from Galilee — the rough, peasant Galilee. It was not hard to guess that this was his first visit to the Holy City.

Nearby two older men were talking. One was balding and fat. The other was heavily bearded and highly animated in his talking. They seemed detached from the crowds. So intent were they in their conversation that a boy walking with a donkey almost knocked down the bearded man but the man did not stop his talk nor his waving arms.

A mother and child come out of a doorway, the child still rubbing sleep from his eyes. Quickly they crossed the square, moving directly to the well. Once there they drew water and returned as quickly to their home. They did not speak to anyone, nor to each other.

From the temple end of the square a royal, robed priest moved through the crowd. Actually the crowd separated so that he had a clear path. He, too, did not speak to anyone. His step had a haughty gait, as if he really did not want to be so close to so many common people.

And there were many others in the square that morning so that the whole square was like a churning pool of water, forever moving, currents forever flowing, in an ebb and flow of humanity.

As one surveyed the noisy, international crowd and looked to all the buildings that framed the square, one structure remained shuttered to the warmth of that new day. Only one. Its two windows were covered with wood planks, fastened to the inside. The door, marked with mud at its base, was closed. It was a door with no outside handle. Once closed and locked within it would remain shut tight. And it remained so all morning.

Then, very suddenly, the closed door burst open. Men were running out of the room, out into the busy, surging square. Some immediately began talking, shouting to those nearby. Others ran toward the well, to the high ledge that marked that part of the square. The one with the loudest voice, and the largest frame, shouted for quiet. Then he told of Jesus, his Lord and Master! And people who you would think could not understand did understand. It was a miracle. It was the birth of the church.

The event of the Christian Pentecost as recorded in the first chapters of Acts describes one way by which God's Holy Spirit took hold of human lives and worked transformation. Scriptures of this Pentecost Season tell additional stories of the Spirit's work, inviting us into that "journey of the spirit."

Each chapter is introduced by an imagined scene. "It might have been this way." These little stories may be used within the sermon or as an introduction by another reader. Perhaps they might be used as a drama, complete with costume. They seek to set the scene for the scripture and sermon.

These chapters are dedicated to one who has shared not only the spiritual journey but the earthly one as well — to my wife, Karen. Through her own study of scripture and through her own professional work in the field of nursing research, she has been both inspiration and companion. My love and admiration — and a sense of the Holy Spirit's guidance and protection — marks this dedication.

— Leonard H. Budd
Cleveland, Ohio
September, 1992

The
Spirit's Tether

Young Amos was a servant boy who, as an orphan, had attached himself to the Galilee travelers. He drew water, did washing, ran errands and always answered to the call, Young Amos. On a special day with that traveling company the intensity of the house was matched only by the heat of the hour. As the disciples remembered it years later, it was as if Jesus was speaking his final teaching. Everything he had tried to convey needed to be packed tightly into his lesson. Jesus kept alluding to a time when he would be gone from them all. The more he talked about it the closer it seemed that moment would be. "I go to the Father," he said. "This is the command I leave with you," were words of introduction to his constant theme of self-giving love. "Now I am going to him who sent me."

Young Amos did not understand it all, except for the heat of the room and the sense of urgency in Jesus' voice. Months later he would understand. Months later he was years older! Months later Jesus was gone from that old disciple band. He had been crucified, declared dead, was buried — only to rise in new consciousness to the very men who had listened so intensely. And Young Amos, in his new growing, was numbered a believer. That promised Counselor was now part of his daily life. That Spirit-presence was a close companion to him in life's experiences — even as the words of Jesus had been to his ears months earlier. Amos was now understanding Jesus' work as he had not understood before. It was work such as God would do. Because of his new understanding, the disciples no longer called him Young Amos. Now, in the life opening to all of them, he was simply Amos, an equal in the special work ahead.

———————

One of the mysteries of your life and mine is how God's spirit can take hold of us, and change us! Everyone here can know that mysterious Presence — that Counselor, as Jesus taught of it — and in that acquaintance can be changed in very blessed ways. One of the great themes that weaves through scripture is the working of this mystery.

I ask you to think of this present force in your own life as the Spirit's tether. Although I'm not a horse person, I do know that a tether is that loose line holding the animal in place. A tether can allow for movement, for choosing this drink of water or that bit of shade, this morsel of grass or that succulent weed. The tether can allow for freedom, but within some guidance, some protection. The tether can allow for standing or lying down, yet the constraints — if properly secured — will not allow for harm to occur. Now in my mind, a tether is the image of the Counselor that Jesus promised. It is the experience of God's Spirit that has been part of my living: the Holy Spirit's tether.

In the scriptural report of Jesus' final conversations with his chosen disciples, the day's lectionary text, he speaks of three ways by which this spiritual tether can be part of our lives. May it be a sort of test! Ask yourself, does God's Holy Spirit affect the person I am in these ways?

The Spirit's tether guides us to recognize sin.

When an inner-city youth takes a gun in hand and shoots another teenager because he wants the teenager's high-style sneakers we see the presence of sin. To think of another's life as so expendable is sin. To be so self-centered is sin. To value material possession over human life is sin. That is the easy recognition. But don't you believe that the Spirit's tether also condemns the conditions of urban rot in which that gun-toting youth came to maturity? There is sin in the societal drive to possess those sneakers, a drive coming at that youth from all sides of our society. There is sin in the lack of parental strength and guidance, maybe even in the lack of parents? The Spirit of God forces us to look through and beyond that exploding gun shot.

As Christians we are called upon to see the sin that is about us, that affects us, that can be part of us — and thus, through us, sin of the world. The headlines of child abuse in affluent homes describes sin, as does child abuse anyplace. Spouse abuse and white collar crime are manifestations of sin just as much as is armed robbery. There is violence in act and word that is sin. We people of the Bible say that "sin raised the cross" upon which Christ was crucified. But such a truthful affirmation is also to recognize that crucifixion takes place in a thousand ways today as then.

God's Holy Spirit guides us to recognize the many individual sins — and the collective sin — that is part of our human story.

The Spirit's tether also allows us to value righteousness. That is the second word Jesus spoke on that special day.

For the last couple of weeks Karen and I have been traveling. On our 2,000-mile vacation sojourn through the lands of our nation's beginnings we came to Highland in Charlottesville, Virginia. It was the home of James Monroe, on a location chosen by his friend and mentor Thomas Jefferson. Highland and Monticello were within signal distance of each other. Throughout his lifetime, James Monroe held more major offices than any other President. He was a senator and minister to England, Spain and France. He negotiated with Napoleon for the Louisiana Purchase. He was governor of Virginia and, at different times, both Secretary of State and War in the Federal government. He was the fifth president of the United States (1817-1825). "The Monroe Doctrine" told the European powers that we meant to keep our independence, and to protect others in our hemisphere so that they might keep theirs. He gave of himself to this country in its formative years. And he saw it as his obligation in life. He died in 1831 — on July 4th.

We drove the winding road from Monticello and parked next to a strutting peacock, then walked up to the front door of Monroe's 19th century plantation farmhouse. He had moved there in 1799, but because of his continual giving of himself to his state and country he did not live there much. In his last years as President he often said that he looked forward to retiring to his cabin castle at Highland. But there is a sad footnote. When he left the presidency after a lifetime of giving of himself for the country, he was broke. We saw the ad he placed in the Charlottesville newspaper, inviting buyers. He had to sell his cabin castle to pay the debts he had incurred as a servant of the people. But he did so without regret.

I suppose we can think of many ways in which good living and righteousness leaves its mark upon life — upon our lives. After our vacation visit, James Monroe's gift of himself to the struggled beginning of this nation becomes one more example. In ways that neither he nor I could fully understand, I think God's Holy Spirit was present.

I tell of it, though, in order that you might think of how a holy righteousness is part of your life. That was part of Jesus' last message to his followers.

The Spirit's tether further calls us to stand under judgment.

How does the Spirit's judgment fall? Let me count the ways — or, at least, mention one? With all the talk of "family values" these days, with talk of morality and ethical behavior, consider but a single teaching by our Lord: "In everything, do to others as you would have them do to you; for this is the law and the prophets." (Matthew 7:12 and Luke 5:31)

How blessed we all could be if that was more universally accepted as a family value, as a moral precept for human behavior. We Christians live under that judgment!

But there is more, I believe, more work by the Spirit, by the Counselor. That Golden Rule is part of every living religion. Listen: Confucianism: "What you don't want done to yourselves, don't do to others." Buddhism: "Hurt not others with that which pains thyself." Plato, speaking Classical Paganism in the 4th century before Jesus: "May I do to others as I would that they should do unto me." Hinduism: "Do naught to others which if done to thee would cause thee pain." Judaism: "What is hateful to yourselves, don't do to your fellowman." Sikhism: "Treat others as thou wouldst be treated thyself."

I think one can say, God's universal spirit holds us in judgment.

When Jesus' earthly ministry was finished he promised that God's presence — God's counsel — would continue to be with his followers. That Holy Spirit reveals sin, empowers righteous living, judges us all. That blessed Holy Counsel is a gift from God. If I could borrow from Karl Malden, "Don't leave home without it!"

There is a poem by Percy Dearmer, an English song writer, that talks of this guiding presence of God. It is a beautiful image of God's Holy Spirit. The tether is the guiding cord. Although it is often a communion hymn, we sing it as our closing hymn now.

> *Draw us in the Spirit's tether;*
> *For when humbly, in thy name,*
> *Two or three are met together,*
> *Thou are in the midst of them:*
> *Touch we now thy garment's hem.*

Living
Water

To call it a "wilderness" is not strong enough, not descriptive enough. That land surrounding the Dead Sea is a wild part of earth, burned by the sun of day and frozen by the winds of night. The rocks of this terrible terrain between the depths of Jericho and the heights of Jerusalem are jagged and up-ended. It is eternally dry.

Jarib had foolishly set out from the Jordan River banks without enough water. The animal skin was only half full as he began his journey. His travel to the high Jerusalem was taking much longer than he expected. The path he followed, instead of always climbing up, was snaking through rock valleys and over rock cliffs and down into rock ravines. Some of the ravines were now dark in shadow. The sun was lowering more quickly than he had expected. His water gone, Jarib was exhausted. Yet, he dared not stop to rest. He stumbled more with each hour. His tongue was swollen, he thought. He licked the sweat from his arm, knowing that he shouldn't. The cold was beginning to blow with the night air, coming up from the dark ravines in the rock. On he walked, and stumbled. His sheep-skin water container had long since been thrown aside. As had his heavy cloak.

If only he could find water. If only a spring would bubble up at his feet. If only a tracing of water could be found on

19

the rock surfaces that surrounded his path. His thirst was over-powering now. He could hear the water just ahead. But it wasn't. Only more rock. Just a handful of water was all he wanted — all he needed. In the increasing darkness he was sure a fast flowing stream was just a few steps ahead. Jarib hurried now — only to step into a darkness that dropped 50 feet. He did not rise when he stopped falling. Nor was there any water in that dry gully miles from Jerusalem's walls.

. It is terrible to thirst and not have the thirst quenched!

And, of course, our thirsting in this life is for more than water. You and I may thirst for all sorts of things and conditions and relationships. Thirst can be for money, more money. Thirst can be for power. Thirst can be for success — success in one's chosen profession, or success in family life, success in just being a well-rounded human being! We all thirst. That is not the issue. The issue is how the thirst is quenched!

Our Lord spoke of this universal need to have one's thirst quenched. His invitation was to find those needs met by coming close to him, learning from him.

"On the last day of the feast," when Jesus spoke his message, "If any one thirst, let him come to me and drink," I wonder if he was remembering back to the time he traveled through Samaria? (John 4) Jews did not like to travel through Samaria — it was half-breed country — but he made that trip. In the travel he stopped to rest by Jacob's well. There, according to Jewish Law, he did a terrible thing. He talked to a woman, a woman who happened to be a Samaritan, a Samaritan woman who was, to put it politely, a "loose woman." She had had five husbands and was now living with a sixth man. In that conversation by the ancient well, Jesus announced himself as "living water," and he invited that loose Samaritan woman to drink deeply of the spiritual water that Jesus offered — the sort of water that can deal with the many thirsts in life, the sort of refreshment that moves on to eternal life. It was an image that was easily appreciated in that dry land of Judea and Samaria.

It is an image that conveys urgency, too. We can get along without food for many weeks. We cannot live longer than one week without water. Biologically, this is our most fundamental need! It is said that at the last, when we are dying, it is the final thing to be thirsty. One of our last powers is to drink. Civilization rests on the ability to have or control water. James Michner's novel, *The Source*, is the moving story of human life through 35 centuries at a single source of water. His story is drawn from the Megiddo dig in northern Israel today. To desire water, to be thirsty, is universal!

That means it involves each of us.

And Jesus takes this universal need, lifting it to the spiritual realm, saying that he can quench our thirst. "If anyone thirst, let him come to me and drink." (John 7:37) As I read the scriptures, Jesus says that as we come to him, as he controls our lives, the thirsts that work upon us are quenched! Christ is our Lord. Christ is our Master. Christ is our Friend. Christ is our Teacher. Christ is our Savior. With Christ in control of our life then our thirsts are satisfied!

Do you have moral questions? Is there a thirsting toward marital infidelity, or a thirsting to try drugs or to steal from the company, or lie to protect an image? Is there a thirsting that weakens you with regard to those treasured family values? Do you have a thirst for money, at all costs? Much of our society today is built out of that thirst. Henry Ford, rumored to be the world's most wealthy man, was asked, "How much money is enough?" He replied, "Just a little more." Is getting money a thirst? Power, money, possessions!

To drink of that Living Water says, "What would Jesus do?" How does his example shape my behavior?

Do you have faith questions? Is there a thirsting for specific belief; a thirst to know with a certainty that cannot be picked away with continual doubt, or cynicism? In our scientific culture we like to have everything tied up in careful packages. But some things just do not package so carefully!

To drink of that Living Water says, "Jesus' trust of his Heavenly Father did not depend on all the answers." His garden prayer, for one. And his cry from the cross.

Do you have a fear of the future? Is there a thirst to have a claim to an eternal home? For some persons this becomes an all-consuming thirst.

To drink of that Living Water says, "Jesus saw all of life — earthly and eternally — in God's good care." Jesus shared his own belief in that "house not made with hands, eternal in the heavens."

Dr. George Buttrick, in his printed sermons while chaplain at Harvard University, wrote: "Whoever lives with Christ has in his heart a spring of water, perennial and inexhaustible; a peace that passes understanding, a joy deeper than all passing joys, a life more abundant than any other life, a power that meets any and all troubles, a perpetual fountain, clean and clear, cool and refreshing."

We have stood where Jesus talked with that Samaritan woman, promising to quench those drives that were for her a loose destruction. We have dipped our hand into the cool waters lifted from Jacob's well, the very well from which she pulled water on that day long ago. And I drank the water, much to the chagrin of a nurse nearby. It was a drink to quench an afternoon thirst. But it brought to mind the larger question of deeper thirst in life. We all have them. And the Christian says that Christ is the one to quench the thirsting.

In the opening story, Jarib did not know where to find the water that he so desperately needed. Through the scriptures, Jesus Christ invites everyone to come to him — spiritually, emotionally, with commitment of mind and heart — and in that tie to discover the "living water" that we so desperately need. By his example, through trust as he lived trust, and in hope we do find our thirsts quenched.

God's Descending Spirit

Even in the room's darkness Rachel's face was seen streaked with tears. She wiped her cheeks with the back of her hand. Rachel had been an un-named disciple since Jesus had first visited her village. They had already celebrated two passovers. It had been that long ago. She was not important in the way that Simon and his brothers were important. She could not speak eloquently, nor command evil spirits to disappear. Nor could she carry her side of debate about the religious law. Also, she was a woman. But Rachel called Jesus her Lord. She considered herself a disciple and traveled with that loyal band up to the Holy City. That meant that she had been in the temple crowd when Jesus debated the rulers. She had been in the shadows of the upper room and in the darkness of the garden. She shared in the horror of crucifixion hill — and in the empty loss the day after. It was just too much for her to accept. "How could God do this," she sobbed.

Now, in the dusk of the first day of a new week she, and the other better known disciples, were learning that God was using even the shameful cross for his purpose. She was learning that by the power of the Spirit-presence there was yet work to do. Rachel's tears of deep grief were becoming others tears — in time, tears of joy.

Back during a time when boys were drafted into the armed service, a devout young man was drafted from a farm in south Georgia and was sent into the army. He had never been but a few miles from his home. Now he was suddenly thrust into a new, highly structured environment. But as he left his home he took with him the Christian faith and practices that had been an important part of his life since childhood. That meant, for him, such things as reading the Bible regularly and kneeling by his bed each night for a time of prayer.

Such overt piety infuriated the rough sergeant who was in charge of the company of recruits. He set about to deliberately humiliate the young Christian. He sought to make the young man's life over into the image of hostility and brute force that he (the sergeant) lived. That sergeant abused the man verbally. He issued him all sorts of unfair treatment. He used every opportunity to harass the soldier. Yet, at no point did the young Georgian resort to "returning evil for evil." He endured all the abuse without a word of complaint. Again and again he found occasion to do kind things for his antagonist.

Late one Saturday night the sergeant came through the barracks three-fourths drunk. On seeing the young man kneeling by his bunk, the sergeant exploded. He shouted, and tried every way he could to distract the boy. When nothing seemed to work, the sergeant took off one of his muddy, heavy boots and threw it at the boy. Sailing across the room it hit the young man on the back of the head. It stunned him so that he fell to the floor. In a moment he regained his composure and without a word resumed his prayer time by the side of his bunk. Further enraged, the sergeant took off the other boot and flung it at the young recruit. It, too, hit the boy, but he did not retaliate in anger. Then the sergeant reeled off a string of oaths and stumbled into his own quarters and to bed.

The next morning when the sergeant awoke with swollen eyes and throbbing head, the first thing he saw were his boots: clean and polished, sitting by his bed. The sight was more than he could take. With tears in his eyes he walked into the barracks, found the young man and said, "What is it with you?

I have done everything in my power to break you. Instead, you have broken me. What do you know that I do not know? What is your secret? What is your power?"

The young boy replied, "God's Spirit!"

That is a story from which afternoon soap operas are made — or used to be made. At its most profound level it is witness to the sensed presence of God in life. That young recruit was giving witness to the unseen things that mattered in his life, spiritual affirmations. He was living out a belief that God is a very real presence in daily life. That witness is the singular purpose of this sermon!

To be such a person, as the Bible defines it, is to be a person touched by God's Holy Spirit. God's Holy Spirit: that mysterious influence that takes human life, buoys it up to heights beyond which it otherwise could not attain. The Holy Spirit: gifting strength when we are prone to weakness. The Holy Spirit: offering moral guidance when we tend to drift. The Holy Spirit: providing courage and trust when we are apt to be afraid and cynical. One writer says, "The Holy Spirit is the NOW-NESS of God." It is the immediate presence, the power of God in the moment. It certainly was for that young recruit.

The scripture text is of a remembrance from Easter evening. In fear the disciples are hiding. In that dark fear, Christ "stood among them." In his presence they are confronted with the peace and power of that Holy Spirit. In a way it can be understood as the transfer of that peace and power that began for Jesus down by the Dead Sea. It was the beginning of his earthly ministry.

Jesus was 30 years old, we suspect. He encountered his cousin, John, in that hot, scrubby, separated, devastated area. John was preaching a call to repentance, inviting people to a change in life. He was marking that interior change with a sacramental washing in the Jordan waters. People came from all over the territory to hear the preacher, and to receive the baptism.

John spoke of the evil that lurks in the hearts of men and women. He spoke of the great calamities that awaited those who did not repent of their evil and return to God's ways. His use of the Jordan waters was a symbol for washing away the past evil, washing away the past lethargy, washing away the past sin! And the crowds responded. They came to him as in an ancient Woodstock! They plunged into the Jordan to have their spirits washed clean. They stepped up on the river's shore newly washed in God's sight!

But John was familiar with the ancient expectations of the people. He knew of the coming Messiah! And he knew that Messiah would not only cleanse, he would also liberate the people — set them free to be what God intended. Messiah would offer a new relationship to God. John saw himself as preparing the way for that Messiah. Into the muddy waters of the Jordan stepped the carpenter from Nazareth. Some accounts of scripture say that John saw him, singled him out. (Matthew, John) In other reports, Jesus is simply part of the crowds that sought baptism in the river's water. (Mark, Luke)

In either case, Jesus was alone in those moments. That is usually the situation, isn't it? Life's biggest moments come internally — inside us, working in such ways that the world outside is unaware! He was there gifted with the Holy Spirit of God. He entered the water as Jesus from Nazareth. He left the river as Jesus the Christ, the anointed One.

But, of course, there is more to the mystery of God's spirit. What became a presence for Jesus was promised to those who followed him. Now that Jesus' earthly ministry is ended, that Spirit is handed on to those who must continue the ministry. John's gospel — in this text — tells of this spiritual baptism being given the frightened disciples the very evening of the Easter affirmation. Other scriptures tell of this gift coming later. "Wait," said Jesus in Luke's remembrance, "Wait for the gift of God's spirit." (Acts 1:4)

And it did come! With that gift the disciples became apostles. The Holy Spirit changed them from learners to teachers, from receivers to givers. And it has continued through the ages, right down to the current moment. It is a gift to you! Life today finds strength and meaning in that Holy Spirit of God.

Do you remember Paul's words, speaking to Christians in Corinth? "In each of us the Spirit is manifested in one particular way, for some useful purpose. One, through the spirit, has the gift of wise speech, while another, by the power of the same spirit, can put the deepest knowledge into words. Another, by the same spirit, is granted faith; another, by the one spirit, gifts of healing and other miraculous powers, another has the gift of prophecy, and another the ability to distinguish true spirits from false, yet another has the gift of ecstatic utterance of different kinds and another the ability to interpret it. But all these gifts are the work of one and the same spirit." (1 Corinthians 12:7-11)

I am not old enough and, I hope, am honest enough, never to presume to say how God's Holy Spirit works. That is mystery. My mortalness is too real to pronounce the Spirit's limits, where its presence is most seen, best seen or not seen. I really cannot preach of where the spirit of God touches you! I do believe that the boy who confronted his army sergeant knew the "nowness" of God for his life. He had received the Holy Spirit in an enduring and empowering way. But that is one boy in one situation.

The witness of the church is that God's Holy Spirit, coming down upon a receptive humanity, works miracles!

John Wesley changed a nation's understanding of the work of God's spirit as he moved across England 250 years ago. He was the little man who found "my heart strangely warmed" by God's Holy Spirit. The Wesleyan openness to the leading of God gave birth to many a human transformation. Two hundred fifty years ago John Wesley, touched by God's Spirit, worked miracles!

And, I believe that about Mother Teresa today. We remember her gentle touch upon the untouchables, upon those persons who would have had only the street curb upon which to die, except for her kindness, her divine caring. God's Holy Spirit came into her life in such ways that community life was sensitized to a great human need. All people of good will see the presence of God's Holy Spirit through her living.

But it is not just for the historic or famous. You and I know that God's spirit has been part of the lives of some good folks whom we have known and continue to know. We thank God for them! There are countless examples of God's spirit within daily life. God's Holy Spirit is reality!

Therefore, the only conclusion to this witness is to call us to be open to the Spirit's leading — to be open to God's descending presence. The only purpose of this preaching is to encourage each of us to move into living in such ways that we may receive and hold that Spirit — to encounter the experiences of living in such ways, with such open-mindedness, that the Holy Spirit may be received. Such is the promise and the power!

Path To
A New Life

The city darkness is very different from the hillside darkness. Out on the hillside, where the shepherds work, the darkness gently settles upon the landscape. It is a quiet dusk that melds into deeper shadows and finally, after so long a stretch of time, becomes the dark in which the stars are the only light. But in the city, the darkness comes as if some giant curtain was suddenly pulled tight, blocking out all illumination. It was in that darkness that Ely slowly made his way home through the maze of Jerusalem's streets. He had played too long, and too far from his home. Now two consequences lay ahead of him. One was the beating he would probably receive in arriving home so late. The other was the problem of getting there!

Ely turned onto cobbled streets that he thought were familiar, sometimes feeling his way along walls that he expected to end in doorways. The darkness was so complete that he imagined he was blindfolded, or that he was like the old blind Joseph that begged near the city gate. At one turn he saw a flicker of light coming toward him. It was light from a lamp held in the hand of a very large man. Ely crouched in a doorway and silently watched as the lamplight approached. The man walked with great care, partly because he did not know the street and partly so as to be as silent as possible. Ely held his breath as the man, lamp in hand, walked by.

When he had gone perhaps 20 paces further, the man hesitated a moment, and then very softly knocked upon a near door. Immediately the door was opened, casting light upon the nighttime visitor. Enough light shone to reveal the quality of robe he wore and a learned face. "He must be a scribe," Ely thought, "a scribe from the temple." The man crossed the doorway, the door shut quickly, leaving the street in that hard darkness of the city. Ely began his journey once again, trying to remember his way through the maze. He surely would remember this night. He did not like to contemplate it further!

So, too, would Nicodemus remember that night. John's gospel tells us of a nighttime visit to Jesus. His visit provides us with, perhaps, the major spiritual lesson taught by Jesus. "Nicodemus, unless one is born of water and the Spirit he cannot enter the kingdom of God. What is born of the flesh is flesh, and that which is born of the Spirit is spirit." (John 3:5) Jesus ended his discussion with this ruler of the Jews with what has been titled, *The Little Gospel.* As John recounts the discussion, Jesus told Nicodemus, "God so loved the world that he gave his only Son, that whoever believes in him should not perish but have eternal life." (John 3:16)

Nicodemus' furtive meeting with Jesus has some important messages:

One message is that there is no age limit for learning deeper messages about life. Nor does community status have anything to do with it! Nicodemus was a "ruler of the people," a man of standing in that community! We assume he was also a man of some years, some maturity. Yet, something was brewing in his mind and heart, and that something took him in his maturity and social standing to Jesus in that evening hour.

Methodism's John Wesley was already 35 years old when he brought himself into contact with the Moravian missionaries in London. Many years earlier he had finished his studies. He had long ago learned history and philosophy and many languages. He had been ordained a priest years earlier. But now, at age 35, he first discovered his spirit-being "strangely warmed." The message of God's love had penetrated his mind in such a way that — with a third of his earthly life already over — he was now a changed person. That personal experience shaped the remaining two-thirds of his years upon this earth. That is what Jesus was talking about when he met with Nicodemus.

The deeper questions of life's meaning can be discussed when one is in the teenage years or the fifth, seventh or ninth decade of life. The deeper aspects of life's meaning can be questioned when one is newly married or much later. The facing of the deeper questions of life's meaning can come from some fiery event — like a plane's crash at takeoff — or can be part of life's routine growing. But questioning the meaning of life is part of every human life; it is part of our growing and deepening as human beings.

One nameless poet gave sly and humorous assent to this grappling with life's deeper meanings with these words:

> *King David and King Solomon*
> *Led merry, merry lives,*
> *With many, many lady friends*
> *And many, many wives;*
> *But when old age crept over them,*
> *With many, many qualms,*
> *King Solomon wrote the Proverbs*
> *And King David wrote the Psalms!*

Nicodemus must have been at that point in his life. He sought out Jesus to talk about important things.

Jesus' word to Nicodemus was the invitation to begin living in a different world. Even as he talked with him about "new birth," he must have been looking at the fine robes that Nicodemus wore. He certainly knew of the social and political power that Nicodemus could wield. From a distant view, Nicodemus was a man of the world who had everything he could want!

But Nicodemus obviously didn't feel that way. And those feelings are not limited to ancient history. There are many persons of wealth, standing, power, education, good looks, who

31

can see themselves in the sandals of this ancient Nicodemus. You may be such a person. You may be one who can sing with Peggy Lee about your life, "Is that all there is?"

Even as the door was opened for the finely robed Nicodemus, so Jesus opened another door for him — a spiritual door, a door opening to a wider world. We are invited to understand that life upon this world is not the full story of life! "Nicodemus, you must be born again. You must be born into the new life, this spiritual understanding of life." I imagine Jesus going on to say that life for Nicodemus is more than temple meetings, more than the rituals of Sabbath, more than the accolades of the crowds that watch the priestly processions, more than many years of age, more than the busyness of life from sunrise to sunset. "Nicodemus, you must start your life again, only in a new realm!"

But this great ruler of the people was so mired in the patterns of sunup to sundown that he didn't understand. "Jesus, look at the size of me? How can I be born again?" You can see Jesus shake his head in disbelief.

God has created us to be more than creatures of earth. God has breathed into us spirits that hunger to be part of the spirit world. It is mystery, like the wind that blows through the trees. We don't understand the wind, where it comes from, where it goes, but we know it is present! It is mystery, this spirit world in which we may be born. Nicodemus, you must enter that new world. Be born again!

Don't fear the term. It has been misused, narrowed and emotionalized beyond helpfulness. James Fowler, as a professor of theology and human development at Emory University in Atlanta, wrote *Becoming Adult, Becoming Christian*. In very helpful ways he writes about Christian conversion:

> *"Conversion means accepting, at a depth of the heart that is truly liberating, that our worth, our value, our grounding as children of God is given as our birthright. It means embracing the conviction that we are known, loved, supported and invited to partnership in being*

with One, who from all eternity intended us and who desires our love and friendship. Conversion means a recentering of our passion . . . . a realignment of our affections, the restructuring of our virtues . . . . Conversion is not so much a negation of our human development as it is a transformation and fulfillment of it.

(P. 140)

Nicodemus, you have to move into this new life as a spiritual being, sensing your eternal value to God!

Then the scripture changes into a preaching mode, as if it is no longer a conversation between two persons in a dimly lit room. Now the conversation is a witness, a preaching, an affirmation of faith. It is the witness that Jesus is present in order to be the doorway into that new life. Jesus is the means whereby Nicodemus — and all of us walking with him — can enter into the heavenly realm of God's eternal love and care! It is a realm of such love because "God so loved the world that he gave his only Son, that whoever believes in him should not perish" — should not be limited to earth and time — "but should have eternal life."

Nicodemus was on the road moving into that spirit world. He had sought Jesus, even if in secret. The gospel story tells more. Nicodemus continued on that spiritual road, for John mentions Nicodemus twice more. Once this nighttime student defended Jesus before his fellow Pharisees. It was a bold stand, taken in the beginning of the plot to have Jesus silenced. And later, as the body of Jesus is removed from the cross, it is Joseph of Arimathea and Nicodemus who care for the burial. John says, "Nicodemus, who had at first come to Jesus by night, also came, bringing a mixture of myrrh and aloes, weighing about a hundred pounds. They took the body of Jesus and wrapped it with the spices in linen cloths, according to the burial custom of the Jews." Yes, the record is there. Nicodemus was born again.

It may be that you today are walking with Nicodemus, and you are standing within the shadowed doorway, seeking to move from what has been your style of living to a new plane of life. It may be that you are now ready to accept the invitation to a much more personal relationship to Jesus Christ. To be "born again" has sometimes been arrogantly used, as a badge of self-righteousness. But when Jesus was talking with Nicodemus he did not mean it that way. And so, we should not accept it that way. To be "born again" is to recognize our spiritual character, and to claim Christ as the One who shapes that character. It is that step which personalizes Jesus Christ for each of us. Jesus Christ is my Lord! He has meaning for me. That meaning shapes my life now and for eternity.

I would be so bold as to say that this may be the day when Jesus' conversation with Nicodemus is really his conversation with you! We know the response that Nicodemus made. What about you? I invite you to use the remaining moments of this service for thought and prayer about that conversation. Perhaps you now pray for God's acceptance of you in new ways. Perhaps you now open your life to Christ's leading in ways that you never have before. Perhaps now is a moment when you are "born again," as you choose to understand that phrase.

If this is that moment, I invite you to mark this moment in your mind and heart. Perhaps the marking will all be inside you and we will not know it until your journey is published — as was John Wesley's description that his "heart was strangely warmed" during the meeting on Aldersgate Street. Perhaps you will choose to remain in the pew when the service ends for further quiet meditation. Or, to come close to the altar at the close of the service. Perhaps only to close your eyes and be alone in spirit with Christ Jesus.

Nicodemus is beyond our reach. But Christ Jesus is not. His word is still fresh, "God so loved the world that he gave his only Son, that whoever believes in him should not perish but have eternal life." That word to Nicodemus is shared with each one of us, to bless us, to save us. Amen.

Our Own
Mountaintop Walk

Matthias was the 13th of the 12 disciples! He had been chosen by lot to fill the 12th spot when Judas had removed himself from the close circle of Jesus' followers. Matthias had followed the crowds down from the Galilee and had been close to all the disciples through much of the teaching years. And so, with the casting of the lots that picked him, Matthias joined the inner circle of disciples.

He was a serious man, trained in the religious law, and certain that Jesus was the expected Messiah. So certain was he that he had literally left his family — they had disowned him! His certainty was affirmed by the words of holy writing that he knew so well, and by the words that he had heard from Jesus' lips and the deeds accomplished by Jesus' touch. "This is our Messiah," he often said. "This is the Lord."

The one regret that burned in his heart was that he was not with the 11 when Jesus, radiant, had appeared to the disciples for a last earthly time. He quizzed the other disciples often. "What did Jesus say on the mountain?" "What did he look like?" "How did he seem to you?" "Was he with you for a long time?" And, most important, "Tell me about his words." The 11 would recount it all, ending with Jesus' direction to "Go to all peoples."

That was exactly what Matthias planned to do! He would do what Jesus had said, even though he had not heard the Lord's voice speak. He would leave the Galilee, he would travel across Judea down to the Sea and he would take a ship to some far place. There he would speak about Jesus the Messiah. He would do what Jesus had asked for he was now one of the 12.

Although it is not known with certainty, tradition says that Matthias was beheaded for his missionary work in Judea.

"In Fourteen Hundred and Ninety-two Columbus sailed the ocean blue!" Recently the world marked the 500th anniversary of Christopher Columbus' adventure in the Santa Maria. As we all now know, he did not end up where he was headed, which is why some native Americans are now called Indians. He did not "discover" a new world because others before him knew of it — some even lived upon it! He did make a lasting connection between the two continents, but his legacy to the populations he visited was not necessarily a blessing. This man from Genoa believed "God granted me the gift of knowledge ... (and) revealed to me that it was feasible to sail ... to the Indies, and placed in me a burning desire to carry out this plan." Columbus set out with a belief that he had tested with his mind, and with a faith to which he was willing to give his life! How many of us can walk in Columbus' shoes? When, on Friday, August 3, 1492, the "Nina, the Pinta, and the Santa Maria," eased away from their moorings at Palos, in southern Spain, Columbus was putting his beliefs and his faith into the realities of life.

Before the reports of his trans-Atlantic travel penetrated the Old World, Spanish coins had stamped upon them an outline of the Straits of Gibraltar. Underneath the outline of the Straits was the Latin inscription *Ne Plus Ultra*. It translates, "No more beyond." It meant that the world ended in the great expansive voids of water beyond the Straits. There was nothing more. But once Columbus returned home and told of what he had seen, of what he had discovered, and once that report was widely shared, then new coins were minted. The inscription was changed to *Plus Ultra*. It translates, "More beyond!"

That is the mountaintop affirmation which came to the disciples in Galilee and the word that ends Matthew's gospel. And those 11 disciples — and we who follow in their footsteps — claim the authority to speak that message to the world! What had been a wall, a great confinement, is now the arch of a great doorway, an entry! It is an entry into much that gives us joy!

Part of the joy is knowledge that the harsh limits of brutality, fear, hate and force are not the ultimate boundaries of human life.

In Jesus' century, no death was more tortuous, brutal, demeaning than that of hanging naked upon a wooden cross and publicly dying of thirst and hunger and sheer exposure. It was cruel. To the Jew it was shameful. It was meant to break every possible quality of human will, and in the end to break the physical body as that last breath was expelled, or that last drop of blood issued. The possibility of crucifixion hung over the head of every human life in that Roman world.

But the reports that emerged out of the first Easter told the amazing, mind-altering story that this perfect machine of death did not end life! The Jesus who had walked through the Garden of Gethsemane now walked in Joseph's garden! The Jesus who taught upon a hillside still taught. His words were vivid and direct — and still life-changing. The power of that resurrection reality for the disciples turned everything around. Life's deep, dark valley was instead a mountaintop!

The great defeat that Roman soldiers were so sure would silence the Nazarene did not end his life. Those who made that discovery shouted that God's power is greater than the world's power! Their shout is now our shout.

There is a beautiful poem that marks this affirmation. It is one of my favorites, and one that has ministered to my life. Edwin Markham wrote:

> *Defeat may serve as well as victory*
> *To shake the soul and let the glory out.*
> *When the great oak is straining in the wind,*

The boughs drink in new beauty, and the trunk
Sends down a deeper root on the windward side.
Only the soul that knows the mighty grief
Can know the mighty rapture. Sorrows come
To stretch out spaces in the heart for joy.

There could not have been a greater grief, nor defeat, than that borne by the disciples as the dark shadows of crucifixion Friday fell upon the beginning week. Every hope they had shared was broken. Every dream they dreamed was shattered. The kingdom that their Lord had introduced was now encased in frightened and hiding Galileans. Peter now knew that even their upcountry accents could get them in trouble. The windows were shuttered. The door was locked from the inside. But then, the discovery was made, "Defeat may serve as well as victory to shake the soul and let the glory out." Defeat became the victory!

In wondrous ways that discovery translates into our living, doesn't it?

The discovery is affirmed in the acts of forgiveness expressed within families that now allow for the joy of family love to be regained.

It is affirmed in the acts of charity and caring that are offered across all sorts of worldly boundaries, and the "walls come tumbling down." As illustration, it is in Bread for the World, a Christian organization seeking to feed the hungry. They report that one of every five children in the world are "at risk of hunger." The affirmation of Easter is in their work, seeking to turn death into life for millions of children in the world.

It is affirmed in the great variety of people and ideas who can come together in one congregation — this one — to study in many church school classes and to work together in deeds of charity. This is all done in Christ, as part of the body of the Risen Lord.

The Spanish coin said *Plus Ultra*. "More beyond." Easter's translation of hope in this world is that God's forces of love are greater than the forces of hate and violence. Christians live in that affirmation.

The Spirit presence of Christ is also an affirmation that the great finality of earth's death is not boundary of the human spirit. "More beyond." The enemy, death, is defeated. "Death where is thy sting," wrote Paul. Christians share that belief. It is belief in something yet unproven, as with Columbus' venture from the port of Palos. It is belief in life eternal, living no longer tied to matters of earth, life no longer limited by a body's breath or a heart's beat. The enemy had always been death. Now, in the resurrection faith, there is more beyond! It remains a mystery, but it is held in the power of faith. And in that faith there is no defeat that can overpower the victory.

Some time ago I read a fascinating story. It may only be a story. It is told, not to articulate history but to underscore the victory faith! Wellington and Napoleon were fighting the battle of Waterloo. It was a decisive battle. Life for many, many persons hinged on its outcome. At last, word was transmitted to London by means of semaphores — a visual code with reflected sunlight spelling out the message letter by letter. A sentry picked up the message from his post atop a great cathedral. Letter by letter he passed on the message to London. The first word was "Wellington." The second word was "defeated."

Suddenly a very dense fog settled in upon the cathedral, making it impossible for the light to penetrate the mists and allow the message forwarded on. The fog grew more dense, and its darkness was mirrored in the hearts of the Londoners who had received the word, "Wellington defeated." It meant that Napoleon had won. The English of London were a conquered people. Hope was gone. Liberty was no more. England was ruled by another.

But as suddenly as it had come, the fog lifted. The sentry returned to his tower, and went back to his duties, feverishly attempting to transmit the whole message. And London saw it — the good news breaking upon the city and telling the full story: "Wellington defeated the enemy!"

Whether the semaphores' message to London is history or fiction, it does convey the truth of Christian faith! That truth is the shout first heard in Joseph's garden as the earliest followers of Christ made the discovery. It is the victory message of Jesus' word to his disciples upon that Galilee mountaintop, and it is the shout heard through the centuries as human life has been understood as life lived in two worlds — one temporal, the other eternal. Even *Newsweek* magazine lists deaths under the heading of "Transition."

It is the victory word uttered by you and others who sense that God's gift of Jesus Christ is to redeem life from death. It is the victory word shared in Jesus' last word to his disciples. After the Easter resurrection, the 11 return to Galilee and to a retreat that was known to all of them — a mountaintop retreat. Jesus is with them. They understand his authority over them, over all the life that God has given. His word is both a direction and a redeeming promise: "All authority in heaven and on earth has been given to me. Go therefore and make disciples of all nations, baptizing them in the name of the Father and of the Son and of the Holy Spirit, and teaching them to obey everything that I have commanded you. And remember, I am with you always, to the end of the age." (Matthew 28:18-20)

It's A Small
World After All

Lately Jude had spent more and more time with his head resting back against the wall, eyes closed, reliving the Galilee years. He had been counted in that select band of followers who moved with Jesus through the quiet country of the Galilee, and then moved with him into the turbulence of Jerusalem. Jude had always been a friendly type, and his friendship within the disciple band was wide and warm. Indeed, one of the nicknames he held was "the hearty one." He had traveled with Simon on some of his journeys, until Simon was himself crucified. Now in his sixth decade of life, and more easily tired, his time was given to the remembering.

This warm summer day he thought of the last times they had all been together. It was in Jerusalem and in the home of — what was his name? — ah, yes, John Mark's home. It was the meal and the Lord had ended that fellowship time with words that then sounded strange: "Do this in remembrance of me!" Jude could see the room now: the candlelamps that cast moving shadows upon everything, the heat of the evening hour and of the bodies that were lounged around the tiny table in the room's center, the good food, the good company and Jesus' words. As he let his mind search back those 30 years he remembered it as their most special time. And, it had ended so quickly, so brutally. But Jesus had understood what was

41

happening. That is why he said the words, and why the remembering was so important.

Jude, "the hearty one," smiled in the remembering and lifted his arm as if to take the cup from Jesus' outstretched hand. As he did so the iron chains rattled and scraped across the floor. Jude remembered his Lord, and that supper with all those good friends. Because of them chains now held him within a prison cell. But that was all right — really — for Jude had been faithful in that remembering through all the years. And, he knew that he and his Lord were still together, still one body as they had been in the Galilee so long ago. It was all right.

Have you visited Disney World? Our family has, and has taken that scenic ride through the "It's a Small World" exhibit. As the little boat floated along, animated cartoon children from all over the world sang the song and danced in native costumes. At the end of the ride we stepped out of the boat with broad smiles upon our face! It is a delightfully entertaining trip. But the melody, the song "It's a Small, Small World," had been tattooed to the mind — never to be forgotten! For days and weeks afterward I sang to myself,

> It's a small world after all.
> It's a small world after all.
> It's a small world after all.
> It's a small, small world!

There! Now you are tattooed!

We do live in that sort of world: a small, small world. That is not a new idea for any of us. And we really do not need Disney's catchy song to remind us of the fact. Yet, in this small, small world we often do not know much about those who live across town, or outside our block, or beyond our floor in the apartment building. We know where Paris is, but we do not know who a Parisian is. We know the location of China, but we do not know a Chinaman. We know the outline of Russia these days, but we really do not know the spirit of the Russians. We have learned the approximate location of the former Yugoslavia, but do we know what the Serbs are like or the Croats? It is a small world, and getting smaller, but that does not automatically mandate keener knowledge of other people, nor build a deeper interest in other nations, nor sensitize a concern for much beyond our own family and tribe.

Yet there is in the faith surrounding Jesus Christ a universal-mindedness. It does not come naturally, for we frighten too easily. But Jesus Christ calls us to be a single body of humanity created in the spiritual image of God. The Episcopalian chaplain at the University of Chicago (Dr. Sam A. Portaro, Jr.), spoke to a gathering in Cleveland. He said that Jesus' own ministry was judged by his universal-mindedness. "It was the scandal of Jesus' inclusiveness . . . that led to his arrest and execution. Jesus would not take sides but struggled always to affirm the wholeness of God's people."

It is that wholeness that can bring us to this moment of the Lord's supper. Today's communion table opened on the otherside of the international dateline, on the Tongo Islands, the Figi Islands, New Zealand and Australia. Christians in those distant places took into their hands the elements of bread and wine, and shared with us the remembrance of our Lord. We are brothers and sisters.

And this communion table will not be closed until that dateline is found once again in the Pacific. One 24-hour revolution will see those sharing in our common humanity moving through this common Christian sacrament of remembrance and renewal. All of us all around the world will remember a dark-skinned easterner who took bread and wine, lifted them to symbolize his willing sacrifice, and then commanded that wherever this act would be done that it would be done sharing his spirit-presence. There is nothing like it anywhere — nothing that has such personal unity expressed.

I ask you to hold in your mind and heart this hour that great company of humanity. You and I are but one small part. Yet the Lord Jesus calls us to see that small part as an essential link in the world-wide fellowship of those created in the spirit-image of God.

Think tenderly of those who welcome new life. A baby is a precious thing of immense potential, the focus of love and caring. That wanted child of tender thought may be white or yellow or black or brown or red. Such joy is not measured in color.

Remember during this communion hour people in prison. For some it is a prison of iron bars and electric alarms. Some folks in this congregation work with them in Christ's name. But for many, many others the prison is poverty — which can be just as binding — or a prison of ignorance, or a prison of fear. Hold in your thought and prayer those who fear to leave their homes at night, or who view any person different from themselves as someone of suspicion. Such fears are prison bars.

In this spiritual moment let us remember persons of other religious faiths. So much of the killing these days seems to be in the name of one religion against another. Christ would weep for such angry division in the human family, even as he wept over a city divided and quarrelsome. If only more of the Protestants and Roman Catholics in Ireland could sup together in Jesus' sacrament. If only more Christians and Jews could share a common cup. If only more Moslems and Jews could break bread together.

In these moments, let us remember children and youth. We have provided them with so much in this nation, lavished out of overflowing abundance. Yet many of them do not think they will have a chance at the good life because of the changes and debts that are now life's story. They have been given so much but, perhaps, robbed of hope. Can we be in handclasp with children and youth in these moments of sacred communion? And they with us?

Let us remember, too, the aged. For some in the fellowship of this communion table life on earth is almost completed. As we drink of the cup and eat of the bread let us remember with love those who have given of themselves, and have now been passed by as the world rushes on. Let not our steps move on without them. They are part of the oneness of this sacrament.

Let us think in this communion time of those persons of earth who may die today because they have no food. We raise money for the hungry but for some it will be too late. A man from the subcontinent of India, on visiting this country for the first time, was asked what surprised him the most about the United States. He said, "The size of your garbage cans."

Think and pray compassionately for the leaders of this world. Whether President or Premier or Secretary General they know burdens beyond our comprehension. In this common moment we would pray God's guidance upon them all — every one.

And let us think of the peoples of the nations, those citizens who support their country because it is their home, their homeland. To speak of home is to speak a universal world. Boundaries are so artificial, mere ink dots upon some paper map. But homeland, that has the pulse of life. Of course, we love our native land. But others do their own, and with the passion we know.

This day the world is at the communion table. Some ignore it, or revile it. But it is a sign of God's love for his world. We are part of it, but only part. We are not in a corner all by ourselves. We are in the middle of life, our life. It is a life shared with more than four billion other persons! It is a small, small world. We must understand that we are not "it," nor are we always right about everything. But here we are, so fortunate, and stewards of the life that God has given us.

We receive the communion with thanksgiving for Jesus Christ our Lord — for his open arms — but we do not receive it alone!

Proper 4 (Common)
Pentecost 2 (Lutheran)
Ordinary Time 9 (Roman Catholic)
Mark 2:23—3:6 (C, RC)
Mark 2:23-28 (L)

The M And M Factor

Caleb was probably the laziest boy in the whole village. At least that was his reputation, although no one had ever done scientific study on the question. Caleb could sit in one position — usually, shaded by a tree and upon a matting of soft grass — for hours. He could sit there and watch the clouds move across the sky from daybreak to sunset. Actually, he was never out of bed at day break so the statement was more for effect than truth!

This day Caleb had chosen to escape his field chores by hiding away in his father's grain field. The grain was high enough so that by lying down he was completely hidden. Only the high-flying birds could see him. Which, of course, did not count in any list of possible ways he might be caught. Caleb had really found his place — his youthful resting place.

But suddenly his leisure was destroyed! Sounds of many voices and many feet disturbed his hideaway. And as the voices came closer so did the foot-falls. It sounded as if an army were coming — an army looking for him, he was sure. But before he could run away, the grain around him was parted by an angry crowd who stopped a few feet from him and began shouting. Crouching very still, Caleb shared in an unexpected encounter between Jesus of Nazareth and the religious leaders of his day. Caleb didn't really mean to be part of it. He was caught in the midst of it. Life just moved along, engulfing him, whether he was lazy or not. He long remembered that meeting in the middle of the grain field.

And whether you want to be involved in it today, you are! That is the point. You may have tucked yourself away, but the world comes to you anyway! And you really have to take sides! And, lest you think I am talking of chocolate-coated candy today, I am not.

It is strange to us now, but religion when Jesus encountered the Pharisees was something to be done. Or, better said, something only to be done. Religion then, symbolized by those Pharisees from Jerusalem, was following the good work rules — careful rules, detailed rules, God-oriented rules. On the sabbath one did not work! To make it clearer, so that no one would misunderstand, work was defined by many, many precise definitions, one of which included harvesting — even harvesting grain one kernel at a time by fingertips! In that day you did religion. That is what pleased God, it was then announced.

"Not!" said Jesus, or words to that effect! Religious faith was more than good works! Elsewhere he talked of the two sides of a cup: the inside and the outer side, the motivation and the deed, the thought and the act. The inner beliefs which gave birth to deeds, as well as the deeds themselves. Jesus taught that adultery was not simply an act. Adultery was initially a thought, a plan, a decision of the mind. I believe part of the revival in religious faith in our generation has been this breaking through externals to touch the inner spirit, the soul, the source of belief and motivation. Religion as external observance is not satisfying, nor life-giving when the pressure of living is intense. But when God's Spirit breaks through the externals, then life is entirely different.

Those Pharisees who had traveled from Jerusalem understood that Jesus' way was very different from their way. It was, they believed, the work of Satan, of God's enemy.

As the debate continued, Jesus tried to argue with logic. He thought that it would be a way to reach those learned teachers from the Holy City. Jesus cited the very writings that the Pharisees understood as holy law. King David ate sacred, holy bread when he and his army was hungry. It was bread reserved only for the priests, but King David recognized the human need before the sacramental. That is scripture. (1 Samuel 21) The sabbath is to provide opportunity for humanity to rest and to have time to meditate upon God. "Sabbath was made for humankind, not men and women for the sabbath." (Mark 2:27)

The Pharisees would have nothing to do with such discussion. They continued to hound him. They watched as Jesus' presence in the synagogue brought strength to a man's withered hand. Jesus saw the Pharisees watching and he tried to reason with them once again. "Tell me, Learned Ones," Jesus said, "is it allowed to do good on sabbath?" Jesus knew that the law said it was all right on the sabbath to rescue a cow that had fallen into a ditch. What about a human life? Mark's gospel shares some emotion in the recounting. He says the Pharisees didn't answer Jesus. Jesus "looked around at them with anger, grieved at their hardness of heart." (This is one of the very few references to Jesus' anger.) And so in the presence of the Pharisees from Jerusalem, and in the presence of God's Holy Spirit working through Jesus, the man's arm was strengthened — on the sabbath! Mark then says that the Pharisees plotted how to destroy Jesus.

That is the scripture for today. Now, the M and M factor! It involves siding with the Pharisees or with Jesus.

The Pharisees said one must do religious work to be worthy of God's love and care, to be accepted by God! They spelled out that work with great precision. It had to be precise so that one could know if God really cared for him. This was the reason for the many, many rules and regulations and law that formed the religion of Jesus' day. "You don't work on the sabbath because God won't like you if you do!" Religion involved things that must be done and must not be done.

But, Jesus taught by example that we may do good work as a response to God's love and care that has already been given to us. The healing of that man's arm in the synagogue on the sabbath was done because God's concern for the man willed a strong arm. Jesus knew the power of God's Spirit and he sought to be a channel for that power wherever it could bring God's blessing and goodness upon life. The arm is strengthened. The lame walk. The blind see. The hungry are fed. The despised are befriended. The dying are brought new life. The invitation is extended by Christ: you may choose to do good deeds, as God does good to you. It is the difference between must and may! That is the M and M factor!

This past week some of the committees of our congregation have been talking about finances for the year ahead. Budgets are being drawn up. Plans are being laid for the pledge time on November 1st. When we get into these discussions I always think of a man I knew in another church 12 years ago. He had been a salesman all his life and in his later years was disabled by blindness. He was not wealthy although his retirement income was adequate for his care. When I would visit with him he would recount stories of past time when he taught Sunday school, when he helped with this church project or that. One of his sons entered Christian ministry and he was very proud of that. He had been involved with many Christian projects in the community, in addition to his local church work. A community house was of special interest. On one of my visits, he produced a check — one that had a number of zeroes on it — and said that he had some money that he really didn't need and he wanted to share it with some special interests. Would I divide it up and pass it on? Then, pausing in a special reverie all his own, he said, "You know, I have been very, very blessed in my life and I don't have to make these gifts. I just want to give to something that will be of some help to others so that they can someday say how lucky they are." It wasn't anything he had to do! There was no must about it! It was a may, a response to the goodness that he had experienced in life — even in his present blindness!

It is more than money. Giving also involves the resources of thought and experience and prayer and time — all those resources over which we are stewards. You may teach a church school class or you may sing in the choir. You may help with meals on wheels. You may build a house for another person or visit an elderly shut-in person. You may call on a visitor to your church or lead a Bible study time. There is in our response to God's goodness no must. It always is only an invitation.

Christian theologians talk of the Prevenient Grace of God. They mean that God's love comes upon us whether we are deserving of that love or not. God's love comes to us as a grace, a gift that we never earned. We never earn it with a long list of good works, nor a long list of unbroken laws. God's love and care is given to us. Jesus shared that in the strength he gave to the man's withered arm — a strength given even amid the sabbath restrictions thought so important. In response to that grace we may pass on the love to others. God's love does not demand it. That is sometimes a difficult concept to grasp. Edwin Markham understood it when he wrote these four lines:

> *Here is the Truth in a little creed,*
> *Enough for all the roads we go:*
> *In Love is all the law we need,*
> *In Christ is all the God we know.*

Have You Confronted Christ?

Simon bar Jacob — Simon, son of Jacob — had just finished the pruning of his olive trees, ending with the three old trees farthest from the road. He was pleased with his work and looked at it for some time, complimenting himself with satisfying grunts. "Job well done!" He turned to look out upon the full olive grove of 57 trees. Each one had received his careful work, talents learned through the years and taught to him by Jacob, his father. But as he looked toward the roadside near the orchard his heart stopped. There, walking into his orchard was an army of people, a larger crowd than he had ever seen. They filled the spaces between the trees. One young child actually swung from an olive branch, nearly breaking it off, Simon was certain!

The crowd filled the lower part of the orchard and circled round so that they all were in sound-reach of the man who now sat upon a ridge of rocks that Simon had gleaned from the soil. Simon began to run toward the crowd, uncertain of what he would do or say but certain of his desire to protect his property, his inheritance of olive trees. He broke into a run and was quickly at the outskirts of the crowd. But his initial fears and anger were quieted when he saw that he knew many of the folks now gathered around the teacher. "They will not hurt my orchard," he thought. "I know them."

And he was right. Although they stayed for most of the day, not one branch was broken. Nor did the young boys climb the trees. Soon Simon was listening to the teacher and sharing in that special moment when Jesus, from nearby Nazareth, taught about God. It was said by those standing with Simon that Jesus' own family was part of the crowd. It was said they had followed him from Nazareth, hoping that he would come back with them and back to the work and into the protection of Nazareth. Jesus was gaining too much attention by the things he did and the words he spoke. He was not as he once had been. His family was worried. But in the press of people Simon never discovered who they were.

What he did discover was that shortly after noon, a silence fell upon the crowd. It was a silence that began along the road's edge and worked its way through the crowd until it reached Jesus. Priests from the temple in Jerusalem had entered the orchard. Their presence brought a hush upon the crowd. Unlike Jesus' family they were easily seen! Their dress was elaborate. Their head wrapping was of finest cloth. Their step was like that of royalty, expecting adulation. The look upon their faces was of great disdain, but edged with fear for they were in a foreign setting. They could not have remembered when they last walked in an olive orchard. Those priests came close to Jesus and the leader pointed a jeweled finger to the teacher's face. "You are possessed by Beelzebub," he said. As if to second the motion, another priest quickly shouted, "The ruler of demons casts out demons!"

Simon bar Jacob — Simon, son of Jacob — remembered the silence of that confrontation that took place amid the ripening trees of his orchard. He was there and he found that he, too, had to decide about Jesus.

Twenty centuries later, you and I share that moment of confrontation. That is the point of this sermon from these verses in Mark's gospel! That is the point of the Christian faith! Each of us is involved in the confrontation.

The confrontation came early and with great force in Jesus' ministry. As Mark tells the story, Jesus had just chosen his disciples. He had just begun his teaching times, and word spread quickly that his touch could heal broken lives. The crowds were eager to hear him and to receive from him. The beginning verse of the text tells of it, "the crowd came together again so that they could not even eat."

That word sped quickly to Jerusalem. Included within that word was the accusation that Jesus' newly-appointed disciples picked grain on the sabbath — they broke the law! — and that Jesus had healed a "withered hand" on the sabbath. -- Again, the law had been broken! Something must be done! The religion of law — only law — was threatened! And so the Pharisees traveled down from their high, holy city. They accused Jesus of being possessed by Satan. Jesus was God's enemy. The gauntlet had been thrown down upon the dusty road in the Galilee! Sides had to be chosen, decisions made.

Jesus countered, if Satan is evil, how can Satan do good? This is schizophrenic! Jesus did not use that word! He did say a kingdom divided against itself cannot stand, which is a fair definition of that word. This was not discussion over some small point of religious law. This was debate over change — great change. Little wonder that Jesus' family wanted to hurry him away to the protection of his home.

Midway into this confrontation Jesus said a very harsh thing. What did he mean when he said, "Whoever blasphemes against the Holy Spirit can never have forgiveness, but is guilty of an eternal sin?" (Mark 3:28-29) One commentator, Halford E. Luccock, noted that this is one of the things he wishes Jesus had never said.

Jesus' statement has produced hard emotional scars upon some sensitive persons. Not many months ago I had a conversation with a man who was deeply disturbed. He was emotionally sick. He needed professional counseling — much more than I could provide. What he continually talked about was his belief that he had committed that eternal sin, that unpardonable sin. He never shared what it was or what he believed it was. "I just can't speak it," he said. It was a thought that he had held since his youth, and for thinking that terrible thought he believed Jesus was condemning him eternally. The whole gospel message was — for him — focused on that single verse, that single eternal condemnation by Jesus. I worry about how such a phrase is taught to young people, to young lives just forming serious religious understandings. Biblical literalists, from their position of self-confidence, refer to it as if that single verse stands all by itself.

But Jesus' word is part of the total confrontation that took place that day. The religiously learned stood before Jesus and condemned him for doing good, because it was done on the Sabbath; condemned his followers for the simple act of plucking heads of grain on the sabbath; condemned the common people of that day for their lack of righteousness because they did not follow the religious law with the exactness that they (the religiously learned) followed it. Indeed, the word pharisee comes from separated ones. Those richly-robed leaders were proud of their separation from the sinful common people, from those contaminated by the world. In their haughty separateness, the Pharisees had become so blind that they called the good works of God to be the works of Satan! "The essence of their sin is callous blindness." *(Cambridge Bible Commentary on Mark*, page 32) "The sin for which there was no forgiveness was just what the scribes were doing when Jesus spoke the words — calling good evil." *(Interpreter's Bible,* Vol. 7, page 693) That religious elite was so caught in pride and self-interest that it labeled what was divine as satanic! That was the sin. The religious ones were so tied up in their sense of religious rules that even great good to human life, taught by Jesus as God's good gift, could be seen only as the act of evil. That, said Jesus, in that moment of confrontation, was unpardonable!

But I find another message in this confrontation. In the sharpness of the words exchanged on that ancient day we may overlook a wonderful spiritual forest because of this single textual tree! Through his deeds and in his word here, Jesus is also affirming the wideness of God's mercy and love and forgiveness! God's forgiveness is part of that great expansive good open to every human life. So much of our human sin and error is redeemable! If only this narrow, myopic sin of the scribes and Pharisees is unpardonable, then so much more is pardonable!

That message is one to be shared far and wide. That is good news. Jesus is saying that there is a release from guilt that is offered. Jesus is saying that there is the possibility of a "new start" with our Heavenly Father. Is that the message of the faith you need to hear today?

Some orders of worship include what is titled Words of Assurance. They are scripture words telling the chance of forgiveness:

> *"The Lord is gracious and merciful, slow to anger and abounding in steadfast love."*
> — Psalm 148:08

> *"If we confess our sins, he is faithful and just, and will forgive our sins and cleanse us from all unrighteousness."*
> — 1 John 1:09

Our confrontation with Jesus Christ opens to each of us the blessed opportunity of forgiveness, and in that unburdening, the opportunity for a new start in our relationship to God and to one another.

I hope and pray that the broken and sick man, burdened beyond his ability to cope by that single verse, was eventually able to see the broader landscape of God's great love and forgiveness — that landscape lived and shared through Jesus Christ. For in that larger land is his hope — and ours!

Pathway To God's Kingdom

Jacob knew nothing of the geography that stretched beyond his farmland to the Great Sea. He did not even know that a Great Sea existed out there, westward beyond his land. He had never been further than half a day's journey from the collection of 15 stone houses that formed his village. Nor did he know anyone who had been further away than those eight or 10 miles. Nor did anyone in his village think much about far-off regions. Jacob only knew of the fields and gentle slopes of land that he could see as he paused in the hard work of seed planting. While he did not know of the far reaching geography, Jacob did know about seedtime and harvest. And he knew his limits!

Once the winter rains had slowed, Jacob would prepare the ground for the planting. But before he started the work he fasted, preparing himself for the task of preparing the land. It was a prescribed rite (Deuteronomy 16:13), ancient and mystical. The farm tool that he used was almost as ancient. It was a thick, heavy tree limb, tipped with iron, given to him by his father years earlier. The donkey pulled it, with Jacob ever forcing it into the earth. Together they would break the clods of earth, turning the grasses inward. His field work took more than the days between two Sabbaths to finish — that with good weather, too. When the ground was broken he would place

59

the carefully stored seed into a bag that he slung over one shoulder. Then, as he walked back and forth across his field, he would "broadcast" that precious seed. Each handful would be thrown with a sweeping swing of his arm. When he reached the far side of his field, the planting was done.

With the tasks completed, Jacob looked to the heavens, but not with the eye of a modern agronomist and meteorologist who could calculate studied prescriptions of soil quality and weather to come. His look was of resignation. He had done his part, the only part he could do. Now God would do the growing. In his understanding, the land he worked was a gift from God! (Deuteronomy 11:8) It did not really belong to him, nor did all the crops that came from his work.

But one day the ordinary routine of farming in Jacob's village was broken. It was broken when the Rabbi came along the path from the Great Sea, from Nazareth although Jacob had not known a Nazareth existed. The Rabbi stopped at Jacob's field to talk and to teach. Jacob remembered that moment for the rest of his life.

Others remembered it, too. Years later they remembered Jesus' seed-teaching in terms of the growing of God's kingdom upon earth. The divine in life grows. The heavenly on earth develops, like a seed growing toward maturity. God's kingdom on earth was a very important part of Jesus' teaching and so, "Come, let us walk in the way of the Lord."

God's kingdom, by that title, is not mentioned in the Old Testament, and is seldom mentioned in the New Testament except in the synoptics. In the gospel of John it is cited only twice. In the book of Acts, describing the beginnings of the Christian church, it is only noted six times. But the kingdom of God is a central part of the synoptic tradition, that collection of preaching found in Matthew, Mark and Luke. Jesus' preaching, as remembered in Matthew, Mark and Luke, is filled with illustrations of God's rule upon earth, God's kingdom.

His teaching is understood as both something about to happen (imminent) and as something already arrived! God's kingdom is imminent as in the Lord's Prayer, "Thy kingdom come, thy will be done on earth as it is in heaven." (Luke 11:02) Jesus also taught us to understand that God's kingdom is already a present reality. He spoke to the Pharisees, "In fact, the kingdom of God is among you." (Luke 17:21) In a paradoxical way, that seems true to life. God's working presence seems always to do with the immediate moment as well as pulling us into a greater fulfillment in the faith. The now is blessed by God. The call of God moves us into greater blessings — ultimately, from the kingdom upon earth to the kingdom of heaven.

Through two parables Jesus taught of this kingdom.

The kingdom of God is mysterious growth. We do not have all the answers, there is always mystery with life, yet that does not keep the kingdom from being a reality. It is like a farmer, Jesus said, who plants the seed and then goes to sleep, goes away someplace, and the life within the seed brings forth the shoots, then the plants, then the harvest. (Mark 4:26-29) How? Even the farmer does not know. It is mysterious growth.

You and I who are parents have seen this mysterious growth as a tiny baby grows through childhood, through youth, and then into the possibilities of adulthood. As I see my children grow, I marvel. Can they be the little babies, so helpless, that once upon a time began life. I suspect that every parent looks at a child in such a wonder.

What we can see in physical growth, and marvel at, is also the story of spiritual growth, and of the growth of God's kingdom! The disciple band that clustered about Jesus revealed that growth. At first they were workmen, toiling at daily tasks. Then they became students, disciples of their Lord. As they grew in understanding about God's kingdom they also misunderstood. They denied knowledge of their confessed Master. In fear, they hid because of him. But as their growth continued they moved out of their hiding to be called, not disciples, but apostles, speakers for their Lord.

This spiritual growth is part of this congregation these days. Through some of the church school classes, through the Bible studies, through our youth group, through the many caring ministries of the people of this church, a spiritual renaissance is marked upon many persons here! It is the kingdom of God, growing in ways we cannot fully comprehend now. All we know is that the seeds, once planted, are growing.

The kingdom of God, in this mysterious growth, becomes something of great worth and service. It is like the tiny mustard seed, when planted, growing into a great bush that is part of the value of nature. Even the birds of the air can use its protection for nesting. (Mark 4:30-32)

I want to tell you an incredible story about the mysterious growth of God's kingdom that resulted in a gift of great worth. It is not, like that of Jacob the farmer, a make-believe story. This is a true story about another Jacob!

On April 18, 1942, into gun-gray sky, sixteen B-25 planes took off from a pitching aircraft-carrier deck and headed for Japan. They were under the command of Jimmy Doolittle. Those 16 planes planned a surprise attack upon the Japanese mainland, as the Japanese had done to Pearl Harbor only five months earlier. Beginning about noon that April 18th they made their strike and then, because of low fuel, continued on to the China mainland. The fuel ran out and in bad weather the planes crashed. Most of those airmen were saved by friendly forces, but two of the planes crashed on Japanese-held land. Both crews were captured. The crew of one plane was killed. The crew of the other plane — plane No. 16 named "Bat Out Of Hell" — was held prisoner throughout the war. One of the five-man crew died in captivity. The others were released a few days after the atomic destruction of Nagasaki on August 9, 1945.

One of the survivors was Jacob DeShazer. He was bombadier of that plane No. 16. DeShazer's three years of captivity was the story of depravation, torture and untreated illness. More than 70 boils covered his body. He became weak from dysentery. From the depth of that hell, he searched for God. He later said, "The way the Japanese treated me I had to turn to Christ. No matter what they did to me, I prayed. I prayed for strength to live. And I prayed for the strength, somehow, to find forgiveness for what they were doing to me."

Somewhere in his youth small seeds of God's work through Jesus Christ had been planted. I do not know that even he could identify the planter or the planting time. It may have been a parent in discussion about God's kingdom present within a human life. It may have been a church school teacher teaching a lesson from the very parables that we study now. It may have been a neighbor, a preacher, a peer in his youth. Somehow, in that mystery of spiritual influence, the seed was planted that allowed Jacob DeShazer to struggle with the mysterious growth of God's kingdom in his own life, a growth that took place in a prison cell! (How God's kingdom grows in times of difficulty, oppression, imprisonment — whether physical or emotional.)

After his release DeShazer became a Christian missionary. For three decades he strove to bring the beliefs of God's kingdom to China and Japan. But that seed continued to grow. In a curious twist, Jacob DeShazer was instrumental in the conversion of Mitsuo Fuchida, the Japanese flier who had led the air attack on Pearl Harbor. In time, Mitsuo Fuchida, himself, became a Christian minister to his people in Japan.

Jesus taught about a tiny seed, once planted, growing in mysterious, unaccountable, ways to become something of great worth to the world. In such a way, he said, God's kingdom is all around us and within us!

Of course, we cannot study Jesus' teaching of God's rule without learning the big message that you and I are centrally involved in it! Jesus believed so strongly that God's kingdom was the means of fulfilling God's creation. That blessed kingdom offers the completion of God's creation, moving from earth to heaven. The kingdom offers all that God desires for us. As we seek to walk close to Jesus we are part of God's work through Jesus — we are within the kingdom. And so the invitation is always given, "Come, let us walk in the way of the Lord!" That invitation is to be very attentive to the days of this week. Every day you are sharing in the planting of seeds of God's love and kingdom. But more, you will receive, this week, the blessing of other plantings. Those blessings are part of the walk, too. Through it all, you are growing toward the harvest time — in your living now, and in your claim to that eternal kingdom of God's great love. It is mystery. It is growth.

Proper 7
Pentecost 5
Ordinary Time 12
Mark 4:35-41

Walking Through A Storm

Simon was in control of the boat. He was the oldest, and besides it was his boat. He had sailed the waters so often, and usually at night because that is when most of the fishing took place. The disciples pushed away from the shore, a shore still crowded with the village people. The sun had set but still cast a warm, red glow over the hillside, over the men, women and children who had come to hear Jesus and to be healed. The sun's glow worked out upon the gently moving sea. It may have been John, the youngster, who was last into the boat. His push was the final one freeing it from the gravel along the shore. Soon a small sail was raised. Soon the noise of the crowd was gone. Soon the rocking sea quieted the men and allowed their Master to dip his head in sleep. Soon the glow of the sun was gone. Soon the stars filled the dark sky. Soon, too, the clouds came with the wind. Soon the gentle waves became a churning and dangerous sea. Simon's voice was not as steady, which quickened a sense of fear among the others. Soon Simon's voice was not even heard, nor hearable.

The dark sky seemed to dip down and touch the waves. The wind from distant Mount Hermon rushed upon the disciples as they frantically lowered the sail and bailed water from the boat's bottom. Light was present only because of the lightning. It cast momentary shadows and lighted the white edges of the waves that rushed against the side of the boat. Those lightning flashes also revealed frightened faces. Even the elder Simon's face showed the terror of the rough sea. Yet, the Master slept, still rocked by the motion of the waters. In the midst of that great danger, the Master was calm in his rest.

The Sea of Galilee is known for its sudden storms. The disciples were in the midst of one and it was greater than they had experienced. They didn't know what to do. Those fishermen of the quiet waters were now in a turbulent storm, fearful for their lives. Those experienced workmen of a calm Galilee now faced something very different. And that makes it our story, too!

———————

At one time or another, all of us are afloat on a troubled sea. Worry. Uncertainty. Tangled troubles. Fear. We want the Master to wake up! We want him to quiet the churning waters that are all around us. We want him to solve our problems! We're seasick with worry, with pain, with tension, with fear. "Wake up, Jesus. We're in trouble. Save us!"

When was that last your cry? Life is not always like a calm sea. We are not always rested by the gentle wake. There is much that disturbs us! Each evening, the television news of our city reports sudden death. In the United States there were 23,000 murders last year. Life comes to a sudden end, with finality and brutality. That feeds our fear!

We are frightened by an unknown future in an ever-changing world. Dr. Elizabeth Tracy, a professor at Case Western Reserve University, reported on the changing family. Only 10 percent of families today are of the traditional variety, with father working, mother at home, and marriage of life-long commitment. In this changing nation, there are 1,300 "step families" formed each day. Dr. Tracy, a teacher of social work, reported that children in step families need at least six years to adapt to the changes that have occurred in their lives! She said, "Average married persons today — because of multiple marriages — have more parents than children!" That is something new for us to handle, and its newness feeds the worry, the fear.

We are afloat on a troubled sea, and we cry out for Jesus to wake up and save us!

We physically hurt! The pain, deep inside that comes upon us in the dark of the night, is fraught with worry. Our bodies are not immune to disease nor aging. Each day might bring a diagnosis we do not want to hear. Nor do we want to hear that health care costs rose twenty-two percent last year! That is a deep problem for some folks. Other people know another health worry, for they are part of the 40 million Americans who have no health insurance! The storms swirl around us.

And, we emotionally hurt! In our fast-paced world we can so easily be cut apart by the words that others speak or the prejudices that slice into great groups of people. We are not all Hollywood starlets, nor built like some Greek god. We are not all brilliant in mind nor quick in speech. We do not all make friends so rapidly, nor bond so easily. The emotional side of life can be for us the same as that storm up on the Galilee Sea. And we cry for Jesus to wake up and make things right!

Mark's gospel tells us that Jesus did just that! He spoke to the storm and it quieted. He said, "Peace. Be still." And, writes Mark, "there was a great calm." In our modern, scientific way of thinking, we do not easily understand all this. Storms upon seas are caused by wind currents, temperature differences and open spaces. A recent news article told of this climatic possibility on the Sea of Galilee, triggered by the winds coming off of Mount Hermon and moving down upon the waters. Storms just are not controlled by someone's shout off the back end of a boat. But that is the recounting that Mark gives — and Matthew (8:18) and Luke. (8:22)

Some students of the Bible and of psychology have suggested that Jesus' word to the wind and rain, giving his witness to God's care, calmed his disciples so that they could then tackle the storm! That may have been Jesus' greater power. He infused those trembling disciples with a calmness to see the storm through. I have seen that happen! I suspect you have, too!

67

I have seen that spirit-word of Jesus take hold of a sobbing and broken woman whose husband had just then been pronounced dead. "Peace. Be still." In ways that I cannot explain, she was empowered to move through the difficult days that his death brought. His death came so suddenly, leaving her with young children and much debt. Later, with grown children around her, she said, "I remembered Jesus' words and I figured he was talking to me."

Another person, upon learning that his employment ceased with the next paycheck, thought of the faith witness, "The Lord is my shepherd, I shall not want." (Psalm 23) It became his theme song through difficult days, but days that he did not walk alone. "That shepherd was, for me, Jesus," he said. "And it was Jesus who taught us not to worry about our life." Indeed, that was Jesus' word upon the hillside, "Therefore I tell you, do not worry about your life, what you will eat or what you will drink, or about your body, what you will wear. Is not life more than food, and the body more than clothing?" (Matthew 6:25) It is a conscious shift of mental emphasis.

The ultimate teaching of Jesus — which Jesus was living out in that storm-tossed boat — was of God's good care! The birds of the air are in God's care. The little children are in God's good care. The ill, the aged, the lonely — all are in God's good care. And when the storm is heavy, even when a cross is lifted to the dark sky, it is Jesus' faith that God's good care is there. It is a conscious shift of emphasis from self to God.

I have known that in my own life. There have been times when things were dark, when it appeared I was ensnared, and when there was no tunnel to the light. Then, in the darkness, came a sense that God would see me through. I did not know how. I could not imagine how! But faith in that care has not let me down. For some here, that is your story, too. One of our hymns gives that faith. It was written by Civilla Martin on a Sunday afternoon. She was ill, bed-bound. Her husband composed the tune later that day. It is, says one book, "a hymn of comfort."

Be not dismayed what e'er betide,
God will take care of you;
Beneath his wings of love abide,
God will take care of you.

"Peace," said Jesus. "Be still!"

But we must understand the role of the messenger as well as the message. For the disciples, the power of the peace came through Jesus' words. For the woman whose husband died, peace came through the persons who shared her grief. For that gentleman out of work it came through one close friend. For me it came through a circle of family and a few friends who shared their faith. At one time or another, each of us must be the Master's voice to someone else in a storm! It is so very comforting to hear the Master talk to the particular sea that is upsetting us. It is nice, and so calming, to hear Christ's word upon our predicament. "Be still!" The disciples were calmed by Jesus. But we also are called to share the word of faith.

Remember a later New Testament story. It was of another disciple, Paul, who spoke words of calm to a frightened man. It was not upon Lake Galilee. It was in a dark prison cell during the hell that followed a night-time earthquake in Philippi! (Acts 16:16-40) Silas and Paul were on a missionary journey, traveling over to the European mainland. They had converted the wealthy woman, Lydia. They had met a slave girl who was earning her master a great fortune by telling fortunes. The slave girl was changed by the work of Paul and Silas, which meant a recession in the economy of her owners. They had the disciples thrown into a Philippian prison. In the dark of night an earthquake broke open the prison gates and the jailer assumed all the prisoners had fled to freedom. In the turbulance of that thought he was about to take his own life. But a voice was heard from the depths of the prison, "Do not harm yourself, for we are all here." It was a word to the jailer as powerful as the words Jesus uttered to the sea. Through the voice of Paul, it was the Master's voice initiating a new life for that jailer.

Part of this spirit-ministry in the midst of the storm is that other persons reach out to touch the hurting life, the worried life, the broken life. It is called caring for one another. And it is a blessing shared through the human family. For Christians it is the expression of Christ in our humanity. For some of us this caring is in boxes of food that this day sail upon another sea on a journey to Moscow. Our caring is rooted in our Lord's faith in his Heavenly Father's caring.

Indeed, the storms of life have, for many persons, been the way by which God has opened new and blessed relationships. The dark cloud does have a silver lining! Someone should write a song about that! On one occasion, my wife and I were flying into Washington, D.C. It was one of those flights that are so common today. To get from point A to point B one must, of necessity, go through point C. Washington D.C. was point C between Cleveland and Orlando. The closer we got to Washington and the lower we flew, the evidence of humanity was all about. Ribbons of roads tied together towns and cities. Great shopping malls nested in acres of asphalt. Row after row of houses were clustered near interstate entrance ramps. And, off in the distance I saw a brilliant light shining. It was like a huge diamond set amid a small pine forest. The sunlight danced as it was reflected back to my window in the plane. As the plane circled around for the approach, those diamond lights continued to send strong beams skyward. What could be producing such brilliance and beauty amid the forest land? As the plane got lower on the approach I saw that it was a junk yard. Those diamonds set amid the pines were the mangled metal and broken glass of humanity's highway wrecks. But still, in the tangle of trouble represented in that junk yard, beauty could be discovered.

The thought crossed my sermonic mind that amid the human pain and worry and fear, with the voice of Christ speaking his faith in God's care, there is to be discovered something of value, even of beauty. Christ said, "Peace. Be still." There was great calm. The fierce sea did not destroy. Life was not lost! The faith held.

70

Living By
Faith And Trust

Jairus' little daughter was the sweetest child in the whole village. Everyone said so. She was slight in build and shy in behavior. And she was kind, more kind than any of the other children. Everyone said that, too. So when she fell ill and could not even venture beyond the framing of the front door of her house everyone in the town was greatly concerned. Her parents were well-respected, for her father was one of the 10 men in town who ruled the synagogue. He had lived within the bounds of the town all his life. If anyone had a problem — any sort of problem — they sought out Jairus. He was kindly, like his daughter, and fair and he knew the holy writings. Many times he had given the advice to pray to Almighty God. "The Lord God will attend to your prayer," he would say. And he believed it.

Now, with his tiny daughter lying motionless upon the pallet in the corner of his house, Jairus was confounded that his prayers did not seem to matter. He, along with the whole town, was in great turmoil of spirit. So, when the word reached him that Jesus was nearby he ran to him, pleading for any help that Jesus might offer. "My little daughter is at the point of death." What father would not be anguished to utter such a sentence?

But amid the anguish that he and his town shared, there was the spirit-flame of hope that still gave some light. "If you touch her, she will be made well!" In that faith Jairus moved with Jesus toward the house, walking through the crowds of women who had already begun the death wails. At the end of their journey, the little 12-year-old daughter walked with them. The faith of Jairus held true.

Let us talk of faith. There was another little girl. She was about eight years of age. She had lived all those years within the loving embrace of the Christian church. Her whole family was involved: mother, father, sister and herself. Within that church family she became acquainted with a lady who lived on her street. They were good friends. The lady was always at the church when the little girl was there. Every Sunday morning they met at church. But the lady's husband was not at church. He was never there. The little girl knew the husband, for she had visited in their home. But she never saw that husband in the church with his wife. One day, in quiet innocence, that little girl asked her lady friend, "Where does your husband go to church?" All the people that little girl knew went to church someplace. The reply was unexpected! "Sweetie," the lady friend replied, "he doesn't go to church anyplace." Then there was a great silence. Finally the little girl, having grasped this new and unexplained information, asked, "Does he cuss?"

That is a true story. I know the little girl. And it is not really a word about the husband who does not attend church. It is an interchange about those of us who do go to church. Expressed in thought and words of an eight-year-old child is a statement about those who do frequent churches. It is a story about the image of a Christian ... the definition of a Christian faith put into everyday action. I invite us all to follow up on that this morning. What is it that makes Christians different? How might we frame a definition?

There are some folks who think that a simple affirmation is all that is necessary. "Do you believe in Jesus?" "Yes, I do!" "Fine, you're a Christian!" With the words, "I believe," or "Jesus is Lord," or "Jesus saves me," then all that is needed has somehow been done. The achievement has been made. Heaven is assured. The lifestyle, the attitudes, the behavior beyond that affirmation do not matter essentially, for the "acceptance of Christ" has assured all that really matters — so some people say.

Back in the Middle Ages it played out as a game. The words of faith were spoken from the deathbed, but not a moment sooner. It made for the best of both worlds, so thought the angler of those Middle Ages. And the Protestant Reformation was born, in part, in response to this simplistic thought that one's religiousness is structured only by an affirmation, a formula of words spoken. Unfortunately, there remains some of that simplistic sentiment today. Religious "code words" do not a Christian make.

Whereas there are some people who think that only a repetition of words is necessary, so there are other folks who think that Jesus' ethical example is the sole key. All that is needed to make the Christian is to be a "little Jesus" in word and action. Do as Jesus did!

This, too, falls far short. If we earnestly seek to duplicate Jesus' earthly behavior we will inevitably meet with failure. The most earnest of saints in past ages have tried this, only to be engulfed in frustration and despair at failure. The Methodist story of John Wesley's search to do better in good deeds, even sailing the Atlantic to convert the American Indians, is the story of this futility. A working Christian faith does not come to birth in trying to mimic Jesus' life.

There must be something beyond the "Good Word Speakers" and the "Good Deed Doers."

The one point of this sermon is that the keystone of Christian faith is a trust in God and in that life that God has given us through Christ Jesus! That is the mark, the clue. That is the ground from which the Christian life grows productive and contented and moral. That is the ground from which faith grows more deeply. This trust in God provides the beginnings for an assurance that the essentials of life do not end with earth's death. This trust in God opens eternity.

Jesus showed this! He lived with such faith and trust in God that nothing could defeat him. It was a faith and trust that prompted his good deeds, out of a shear gratitude to God for the gift of life. It was a faith and trust that carried him through trials and rejections. It was a faith and trust that opened to him the windows of eternity. In a moment of fear upon the heavy seas of Galilee, Jesus slept in the back of the boat. Later he quieted the fears of those distraught and sweating disciples. (Mark 4:35-41)

Jesus taught this! Standing on the edge of some Galilean field he said, "Consider the lilies of the field; they do not work, they do not spin, yet I tell you even Solomon in all his splendor was not attired like one of these . . . But if that is how God clothes the grass of the fields . . . will God not all the more clothe you? How little faith (trust) you have." (Matthew 5:28) How do you answer?

Is not this trust in God the root of Jesus' statement that each one of us must take on certain child-like qualities if we would inherit the good that God has provided for us? I read his teaching, "You must have the trust of a little child before God's kingdom can come to you."

The text today is about a man who faced a great, great difficulty. It was a potential tragedy that few persons have to face — the death of his child. While Mark's gospel does not give us a clinical report on the illness or the recovery, what is very clear is that Jairus' faith in Jesus and the Lord God that Jesus proclaimed told him that his daughter would be made well. It was not a half-hearted faith. Scripture says that Jairus asked Jesus, "Come and lay your hands on her, so that she may be made well and live." (5:23) It was a strong expectation of Jesus' power. It was the same faith held by that nameless woman who interrupted their journey to the little girl. She was a woman who believed that with just one touch of Jesus' garment she would be healed. And, it happened! Jesus responded, "Woman, your faith, your trust has cured you." (5:34)

It was this sort of faith and trust in God's care that empowered Jesus' first disciples. Paul would soon write: "We are troubled on every side, yet not distressed. We are perplexed, but not in despair; persecuted, but not forsaken; cast down, but not destroyed." (2 Corinthians 4:08) Is that your faith . . . your trust?

The early writing of the church gave some formal definitions: "Faith gives substances to our hopes. Makes us certain of realities that we do not see." (Hebrews 11:01) And, in the next chapter of Hebrews, the writing directs that we must "throw off every encumbrance, weight; and run with resolution the race set for us." (Hebrews 12:01) Encumbrances diminish faith. Fear diminishes faith. Hate, too, is a weight upon us, as is worry and distrust. And so the message comes at us from many directions: Have faith in God's care. Trust God and the life God has given in Christ Jesus.

Yet, there are some folks, some we know, who have little or no trust, whose lives are filled with complaint and bitterness. Even the American Medical Association says that will kill you!

An old southern evangelist was preaching up a storm and ended his long sermon by asking the people to come to the front of the church and give testimony to what God had done for them. People responded, speaking their strong and positive testimony, but not enough of them to the liking of the evangelist. So, he began to call upon them by name. "Brother Smith, what has God done for you?" Finally he got down to Uncle Harry, an old man, sitting to the side, crippled up with all sorts of ailments, blind in one eye, hard of hearing. "Uncle Harry," he shouted, "what has the Lord done for you?" Uncle Harry laboriously raised himself with the help of his cane and the pew in front, looked up at the evangelist, and shouted back, "Well, he's just about done me in!" There are some folks, far less troubled than Uncle Harry, who claim to be Christian yet concentrate on that same done-in condition. But that is not the message of faith from the Bible, even when spoken by Uncle Harry from the pew of a church.

We seek to hold faith, trust in God and the life through Christ that God has given.

Not far from this place is a woman friend of mine who is crippled beyond imagination. She is alone most of the day and very helpless. Only with a large-button telephone by her side can she call for help. She lives in a country setting. But her witness is that she is not alone. She has a faith and trust in God who cares for her in spirit. Those who volunteer to help her from time to time admit that she helps them far more ... because of her faith and trust in God.

In the late evening in a hospital I prayed with a man about to undergo cancer surgery. He did not have any idea how it would turn out that next morning. As we held hands during those moments of prayer, he said, "I don't worry. I have always known that life is a gift to me. I have always believed in God's care. I have no reason to change my mind now, no matter what happens tomorrow."

I read of a man who died and left his possessions to his children. The heritage was carefully listed in the will. But a final paragraph made that will different from most others. This is what he had written: "I desire also to bequeath to my children and their families my testimony to the truth and preciousness of the gospel of Jesus Christ. This heritage of the Christian faith, received in unbroken line from the apostles and prophets and martyrs, is of infinitely more value than any house or automobile or land or material possession. I hereby bequeath it to them all." Trust in God and the life that God has given through Christ. Is that you?

Beloved brothers and sisters in Christ: the message is, seek to live by faith and trust in God. That is the mark. In that, the Christian life is found ... and it is very good!

Walking
The Familiar

There was still a slick of morning moisture covering the path into the town as Eli and Samuel walked by Nathan's orchard, crossed the small stream, and finished the prescribed sabbath day's journey to the synagogue: in length, 2,000 cubits. By our modern standard of travel it was not far. It was about 1,000 yards. They walked at hurried pace. Their prayer shawls were pulled tightly around them, which helped protect them from the morning chill. Sabbath. The day of rest. In Nazareth the gathering was a comfortable event. Everyone knew everyone, and most knew what the others would do or say, such as the fact that Eli and Samuel were always the last to take their seats. The complaints, the prayers, the remembered verses of the holy writings, it all unfolded each seventh day as if written in some careful text. Eli and Samuel lived the farthest from the synagogue and so it was expected that they would be the last to arrive. They always were. The path they took was so familiar that even Samuel could have walked it alone. And Samuel was blind.

This day as the familiar men of Nazareth sat in their accustomed places, and as the anticipated words were said, and as the routine of sabbath moved along its appointed course, it all was broken by the words of a young workman. The young carpenter, now turned traveling preacher, spoke up in the

77

midst of the sabbath synagogue routine. He spoke up, as he never had done before, with quotations from ancient prophets seldom heard within that place. He left the very vivid impression that he was not just talking ancient words. He spoke with eloquence and with directness. Even blind Samuel cocked his head in a way that showed his attention! And there was a frown upon his brow! With the words spoken by the carpenter, the comfortable routines of sabbath and the ordinary expectations of the town folk had been broken! Samuel leaned toward Eli and with a voice heard by more than Eli, said, "Who is this person to speak so? What right does he have to voice such words here in our synagogue?" Eli whispered back some of the things he had heard about Jesus. Others joined in the recounting. But their reports were couched in modern tabloid words, not in holy words nor in words spoken like the honored scribes.

They just did not like the ease of their sabbath broken. They liked the routines which brought comfort in ways they could not articulate. Something was different here. Something new! And frankly, they did not like it. This new preacher in their midst was just the carpenter, the son of Mary. His brothers and sisters were known throughout Nazareth. Nice people — all of them. But he should not speak so forthrightly! It was not seemly on this nice sabbath day to break from the comfortable traditions. And so that congregation in Nazareth took offense at Jesus.

The little imagined story of Eli and Samuel is to bring us to the scripture, a story to describe some of the humanness of that day when Jesus entered the hometown synagogue and scored a zero. Mark's gospel, as well as Matthew's, does not tell what Jesus said when he spoke in his hometown synagogue. Luke's gospel does. Luke tells that he read these words from the sacred scroll of the prophet Isaiah:

> *The Spirit of the Lord is upon me, because he has anointed me to bring good news to the poor. He has sent*

*me to proclaim release to the captives and recovery of
sight to the blind, to let the oppressed go free, to proclaim
the year of the Lord's favor!*

— Isaiah 61:1

Mark does tell that this visit comes midway in Jesus' ministry. Jesus was heralded as a great teacher and healer throughout the region, except in his hometown. In Mark, the verses
immediately preceding today's scripture tell of the wonderment
in restoring life to Jairus' young daughter. And there were other
healings, and great words of teaching. Now Jesus is back home
in Nazareth. It is the sabbath. Jesus is in the synagogue par-
ticipating as a man of the faith. But "they took offense at
him." Those are Mark's words!

The people attending synagogue that day were so caught
up in looking backward that they could not look into the future. Jesus was still only the child of former days, and the people were so stilted in the rote of the service, that they just could
not understand anything new. And so "they took offense at
him."

Jesus "marveled at their unbelief." Those, too, are Mark's
words. This rejection in his hometown pushed aside any possibility of new understanding of Jesus, and of the good news
he spoke.

With this rejection in Nazareth, Jesus now turns to a new
pattern of mission. He sends out the disciples two by two. They
are to go where they will be accepted! They are to speak the
good news and do the good deeds that Jesus himself set out
to do. The words they all were to speak were words about
repentance, which means, "turn about, change the direction
of your life!" The deeds were the charity of healing, of making whole, lives that were broken or limited. These verses mark
Jesus' first rejection, and his first organized mission endeavor
fueled by that rejection. It all happened because, in his
hometown, the folks were short-sighted, and were so tied to
the familiar, the ordinary.

Thus far, we have talked of ancient happenings. Let us bring Eli and Samuel, and others of that congregation, into our day! For me these verses speak both a warning and a wonderment.

The warning is that we can let routines hide God from our sight. The comfort of routines can hinder the work of God.

I recently heard a beautiful new hymn from Korean translation. Americans are not familiar with the tune, nor with the words. It breaks the comfortable tradition of familiar hymns. How might you react to that hymn? Would its newness become so overwhelming that the words were unheard? Would its tricky tune quickly end your attempts at singing? Or, would the very fact of its newness focus your attention upon it! Could God use the new tune and the new verse to speak to you?

> Come back quickly to the Lord,
> just come back to the Lord.
> Our Lord waits every day
> with his doors kept open wide.
> He is anxiously waiting for you
> every day and every night.

It was written during the Second World War by a Korean Christian, Young Taik Chun. It was translated into English by his granddaughter. I suspect that the Nazareth synagogue congregation would not have liked that intrusion into the so-familiar of the worship time.

We do back away from change. We even take offense at it, sometimes. There is a story floating around about a pastor who gave his annual give-up-something-for-Lent sermon. He pastored a small church in the northern part of our country. Early March was a chilly time, if not down right cold! He ended his sermon saying, "As an example of penitence to the rest of the community, this congregation will worship in an unheated church for the whole of Lent!" As the parishioners made their way out into the damp, late winter chill, the pastor asked one of the members, "Ah, Mrs. James, and what have you decided to give up for Lent?" She replied, "Church!"

Yes, we can let the comfort of ordinary routines hide God's working in our midst. The warning is that we can miss something that may be for us life-saving!

The wonderment is that God does use the ordinary and routine to fulfill divine purposes. Consider your own life. Look at all the routines that fill the days and weeks. The getting up for work each day. The responsibilities of carting the kids around. The shopping and dish doing and grass cutting and letter writing. God works within the everyday activities to bless us, and to fulfill divine purposes.

Each February some newspaper or magazine reproduces an old cartoon drawing of two farmers talking over a split-rail fence. Off in the distance is a small log cabin, with chimney smoke trailing into the sky. There is a date written at the top of the drawing: 1809. One farmer says, "What's new out your way?" The reply, "Aw, nothing much, except that Tom and Nancy Lincoln had a little baby last week." We need the reminder: God uses the ordinary for his purposes.

The rejection of Jesus in Nazareth initiated the first missionary thrust. What had been one voice now was 12 plus one. What had been one healing touch now was 12 plus one. Further, we often think that God's work must be through such grand events as the sun standing still, or the Red Sea being pushed aside. That may be, but much more God works in the ordinary, the routine, the undramatic.

Red Skelton told this story from the stage of the Palladium in London. He said there was a terrible flood in Louisiana. The water rose so quickly that a man had no time to escape and climbed to the roof of his house. As he perched on the house top and as the waters reached his ankles, a man in a rowboat came by. "Can I help you?" he shouted from the boat. "No," said the man, "the Lord will take care of me." Soon the water was at his waist. A second boat came by. Again the offer of help. Again the reply, "No, the Lord will take care of me." Not long after that, the water had risen to his neck. A helicopter whirled into view. The stranded man shouted, "Go on. God will take care of me." Well, he drowned and went to heaven. Once through the pearly gates he asked the Lord, "I've been faithful. What happened? Why didn't you save me?" The Lord replied, "Well, I really don't know what happened. I sent two rowboats and a helicopter!"

That is a funny story, but it translates into some very unfunny realities about God's saving work through the ordinary.

At a meeting of a children's home board, mention was made of how the home was helping a little, unnamed child cope with the severe sexual abuse he had been subjected to by his parents. How very, very sad are the reports of child abuse by parents. Some parents cover their abuse, thinking of it in religious terms! You and I understand that the routine, ordinary, humdrum activity of being a parent should be the arena in which God is at work for the good nurturing of children! Your role as a parent, a grandparent, is doing the work of God! The nurture you provide is part of the working of God. That divine nurturing consists of the simple, ordinary human qualities of love and encouragement and steadfastness and interest. Almost anyone can provide it, sensing that God is at work in the ordinary and the routine. From those ordinary human characteristics, through that children's home, God is mending that little eight-year-old child. Ten billion dollars could not replace the ordinary tasks of human caring and love. I wonder how many other children are abused because of parents who do not provide the ordinary, simple gifts of love, attention, encouragement and steadfastness.

The wonderment is that God can use us in the midst of the routines of every day. God can mend and heal and make whole lives right in the midst of ordinary circumstances. And thus we are part of that extension begun by Jesus when he sent out his disciples two by two. You and I are part of that company that speaks of God's love for us and for all his children.

The warning: We can miss God at work in our midst when we cling so unthinkingly to old and hard routines. The wonderment: God does continue to work his way in our midst through those ordinary routines. Where is the Lord God speaking to you through the routines of your living, through the ordinary? Samuel and Eli, and that synagogue in Nazareth, did not understand. Let us not walk in their shoes! Instead, "Come, let us walk in the way of the Lord." Amen!

Proper 10
Pentecost 8
Ordinary Time 15
Mark 6:14-29 (C)
Mark 6:7-13 (L, RC)

A Solitary
Witness

The raw skin on Marcus' ankle was still bleeding as he began work in Herod's palace. Never mind that the chains had rubbed raw the young skin. Never mind that the healing would take time, and would leave a life-long scar. Never mind that the cut, extending clear around his ankle, hurt with each step. Marcus was a slave. One did not have such concerns about slaves. They were expendable, like the clay tablets that the money counters used.

And, even if someone did care about the new slave, there were much more important things to think about. Herod's palace had been in an uproar since the jailing of the preacher, John. Nothing, it seemed, would silence this Jewish preacher. His wild dress drew the crowds, and his condemnation of Herod had become quite fashionable. And so, with slave chains, he was put into the prison of the palace. There he languished until one evening when young Marcus was called upon to bring the severed head of the preacher into the very presence of Herod! Marcus had seen much brutality in his young life. He was very familiar with violent death. But this gruesome task was beyond anything he had experienced.

Herod was drunk. His dinner party had long since become a shouting match between himself and his wife. As reported in the slave quarters, the great king had made a promise to his wife's daughter — a promise he had to keep. It was thought he wanted to retreat from it, but he had spoken the words. Once the words were spoken he could not take them back. Others had heard. And so Marcus the slave, with bleeding ankle, carried the head of John the Baptist into the presence of the king. It was a terrible moment, a moment that Marcus remembered all his days.

It can be a terrible thing to be held by the words of a promise.

———————————

Or it can be a wonderful thing!

This very familiar scripture story of King Herod's promise becomes a negative text from which a positive message may grow! I center our thought on verse 26 of the text. Herod made a promise in front of his family, his peers, his court. In his perceived position, in his arrogance, he discovered that he must hold to his promise. The words had been spoken. Because of those words, John the Baptist was beheaded.

Now verse 26 also speaks of another sort of word spoken. The Christian's commitment to Jesus Christ is a promise. Sometimes it is made before our family and peers. Always it is a promise made before God! The steadfastness of that promise is a very wonderful thing. It is like living water. It is like a house built on a rock. It is like putting on the whole armor of God.

But let another story tell of the power of the promise. This one is a true story.

St. Radegund is a very tiny village in Austria, edged against the German borderland. It is hard to find. It is not on many maps. It is so small there is no post office in St. Radegund. In that little village there is a tiny church, perched high over the river dividing Germany and Austria. Next to that tiny church is a graveyard. Within the grounds is a grave holding the ashes of a farmer. He was a very simple man. His life was undistinguished as the world seems to judge lives, except that in 1943 that peasant farmer, a father of three little children, was taken away to die in Berlin. There is a wooden cross over the grave and upon the cross is the name, Franz Jagerstatter.

Franz Jagerstatter was born in 1907. He was a farmer. He had no schooling beyond the fifth grade. His father was killed in a battle of the First World War. Franz grew up as a very average youth. He had a loud motorcycle of which he was very proud. He was once fined for his involvement in a fistfight with a group of youth from a neighboring village. It may be that he fathered a child out of wedlock, as he himself was born out of wedlock.

His friends and neighbors were surprised to learn that Franz, in his early 20s, enrolled in voluntary religious classes conducted by the pastor of St. Radegund. By the end of that decade of his life a change had occurred. It was a change that those close to him said was "sudden and total." "It was," said a neighbor, "as if he had been possessed by a higher power." Now he never passed a church without stopping in for meditation. Now he was sometimes noticed interrupting his labor in the field in order to pray. For a time he thought about joining a religious community, but ultimately he decided in favor of family life and farming. He married in 1936. He and his bride honeymooned with a trip to Rome. The children arrived: three little girls.

With his religious awakening came a deepened social concern. He saw the essential godlessness of the growing Nazi movement. His praying grew longer and more intense. In 1938, when Austrians voted in favor of national annexation with Nazi Germany, Franz resisted. He spoke out against the plan. He received pressure from the pastor, the mayor and many neighbors. "Don't call attention to our village," he was warned by all, "for our voting can change nothing." Still, he cast the village's only dissenting vote.

In the summer of that same year he had a remarkable dream. His words described it: "I saw a beautiful, shining railroad train that circled around a mountain. Streams of children, and adults as well, rushed toward the train and could not be held back." In his dream he heard a voice say the train was going to hell. It became clear in his mind that the train was Nazism; that he and every citizen of that Third Reich were among the passengers. He had to make a choice between his religious faith and the political order. To choose his faith would require a means of resistance. "I would like to call out to everyone," he wrote in his journal, "jump out of the train before it reaches its destination, even if it costs your life!"

Like every able-bodied Austrian man, Jagerstatter was called to military service. His draft notice arrived in February 1943. His oldest daughter was five. He sought spiritual counsel. "What does God want me to do?" Here was, for him, a meeting of the spirit world and the temporal world. Ignoring the advice of his pastor and many others, he refused to take the military oath. His promise had been to Someone else. For this he was immediately jailed. He was offered non-combatant service. He refused. It would still mean that he must wear the uniform.

In pencil on the pages of an ordinary composition book he asked himself, "For what purpose, then, did God endow all men with reason and free will if, in spite of this, we are obliged to render blind obedience?" And, he wrote some letters from his prison cell. "Just as the one who thinks only of this world does everything possible to make life here easier and better, so must we too, who believe in the eternal kingdom, risk everything in order to receive a great reward there."

He wrote: "The surest mark [of the follower of Jesus] is found in deeds showing love of neighbor. To do to one's neighbor what one would desire for oneself is more than merely not doing to others what one would not want done to oneself. Let us love our enemies, bless those who curse us, pray for those who persecute us. For love will conquer and endure for eternity. And happy are they who live and die in God's love."

This was practiced, even in the prison cell. The prison chaplain in Berlin (Dean Kreuzberg) said later, "I can say with certainty that this simple man is the only saint I have ever met in my lifetime."

On June 6, 1943, Franz Jagerstatter was found guilty of "undermining the military power" and sentenced to death. New attempts were made to save his life. His wife and the young priest who had replaced his exiled pastor journeyed to Berlin to see him. As they talked with him, they could see traces of the hunger and abuse he was undergoing. They talked of "duty," of "only following orders," of the state's "authority," of the fact that his solitary actions would ultimately mean nothing. He replied that he did not wish to be guilty of any injustice, he could not take even the slightest part in it. They left the prison and Berlin with the assurance that he was happy to have come so far without weakening, and that he was confident he could continue so to the end.

The court's sentence was fulfilled. Franz Jagerstatter was beheaded. He was not yet 37 years old. The date was August 9, 1944. Just before his death, he wrote, "I am convinced that it is best that I speak the truth even if it costs me my life."

A few people called him a martyr. In 1987 a memorial mass was conducted in Linz, Austria, culminating a three-day observance that would have been his 80th birthday. Other people have called him a deserter. They cited his family responsibilities. They said his act became a condemnation upon all those who did not express a conscientious objection. Still other people saw it only as a senseless waste of human life.

Historian Reinhold Schneider wrote: "When the commission of sin [intersects] one's sacred duty, there remains nothing else to do but to refuse and thus to bear witness, even solitary witness. But where such witness is, there is the kingdom of God!"

Each one of us is involved in "solitary witness." It is because of a promise made, perhaps in front of friends and family, but always before God. The promise and the witness will not take us to the beheading block. But it will determine our course in life. Franz Jagerstatter saw his life as more than being a peasant farmer from St. Radegund. He saw his life as more than a span of years upon earth. In that vision he touched the core of religion. Of course, martyrs are made from such stuff. But so are you and I! That is the message of promises to be kept, even from such a person as King Herod!

The Compassionate Highway

Her name was Mary. Quite a common name. She lived in a village near Capernaum, a village of fishermen who worked Lake Galilee through the night hours. Mary was childless and unmarried. She was cared for by her older brother, who was more like her father in that he was twice her age. She was 18. Her brother was 36 although ages were not kept in that ancient day nor in that little village. Her brother was simply one of the elders, an old man. And Mary was the sister that he must care for. She was a sweet person, kind and loving. And pretty, too. Also, she was a cripple. One leg was shorter than the other and so she did not walk very much, which meant that she was fatter than most 18-year-olds. She had so little exercise. Sometimes she would walk short distances, but it was difficult for her. Therefore she just sat and talked with those who walked by. Her name was Mary. Quite a common name. And that is about it! Except that one day her brother carried her on his back all the way to the next village. And there, on a bright spring afternoon, Jesus touched her leg and, looking intently into her eyes, said, "Mary, you can walk!" Later that afternoon, that wonderful afternoon, Mary walked back to her own village. She walked slowly, and with some pain, but she was not carried by her brother. She walked, and her life was never again as it had been!

That is a make-believe story. Still, I ask you to remember Mary, for she is really us! Our name is Mary.

Two bits of the gospel story are put together for today's lectionary lesson from Mark. First (6:30-34), the disciples have been out in the neighborhood, teaching the words that Jesus had taught them and doing the good deeds that they had seen him do. You remember that, after his rejection in Nazareth, he commissioned his close followers to be his messengers to the world. Now they have returned to Jesus with reports of their work. I suppose we might even say, in today's images, that the sales force is back at general headquarters. The calls have been made. The results are being tallied. But, unlike some of today's images, Jesus is deeply aware of the emotional drain upon his friends. It must have been evident to Jesus that the disciples had traveled far, had been diligent in their teaching, and had given unstintingly of themselves in their healing of life's hurts. Now, together again, Jesus says it is time for rest, time to recharge the batteries!

Dr. William Barclay, in his commentary on this part of Mark, says that these words of scripture describe "the rhythm of the Christian life." It is not possible to be all that Christ asks us to be without moments of retreat and renewal. It is not possible to be all of the time at the tasks of feeding the hungry and healing the ill and clothing the naked and comforting the dying — without stepping back into times of renewing our resources. Burnout can happen to church workers as well as to those in the teaching profession or in sales. Occasionally I worry about some folks who are the good deed doers in local churches. They assume so many worthy responsibilities and carry out the tasks so conscientiously that there may come the day when they must back away to restore their resources. If they do not, they can break! That break does not serve the Master's purpose, nor build his kingdom.

Jesus proposed that spiritual restoring by trying to take a boat to the other side of the Galilee Lake. He and his disciples were headed for a lonely place. That is not only an ancient

92

practice. I have a friend in ministry who annually goes to a Roman Catholic monastery in another state for such retreat. There he has a room, a cot, a chair and desk and the chapel bells that sound every three hours, inviting him to times of thoughtful meditation. In that place, he is separated from the intensity of his daily work. From that place, alone he is resourced to better enter the intensity of ministry once again. Also, I found the high mountains of Colorado to be such a time for me. It is nice to have a wife who must take business trips and allows her spouse to come along! It is helpful for more than priests and ministers! It is the sort of help provided to a young mother by a mother's morning out. It is the sort of help provided by going to a ball game, or, I am told by someone close to me, by going shopping at the mall! We do need that rhythm in our lives that backs us away from the pressure and allows us the time apart for strength-gaining.

Of course, the most obvious (and least understood) time for such spiritual strength-gaining is what we are about at this hour! We come to the sanctuary, the sacred place set apart, in order that we might be blessed, forgiven, recharged for the opportunities of ministry that call to all of us when we leave this place. One old Colonial church had upon its front door's lintel, on the outside, the words, "Come to worship God." The same lintel, on the inside, said, "Leave to serve God's children." Both directions are necessary. I find that so in my life. I hope you do, too! Poet Mary Hallet knew this when she wrote:

Until I caught the rhythm of [Christ's] life,
I had not heard the music of the spheres,
The simple cadences of ancient psalms,
The lyric beauty of a thousand years.

Yet, even as Jesus and the disciples sought the solitude, that sanctuary on the other side of the lake, the plight of the crowd was very evident. You can picture it geographically.

Jesus and the disciples left the people at one point on the Galilee shoreline. They took the boat across, but the people saw the direction they were sailing. They followed the boat, running along the shoreline. With little wind upon the sea to speed the boat, the crowds met the tired Jesus and the tired disciples as their boat was beached upon the far shore.

What should they do? What would you do? This scripture gives a wonderful little window into Jesus' psyche. Despite the need for rest, he is "moved to the depths of his being with pity for them." Those are Mark's words. There was such compassion about Jesus. The image is of a shepherd sensing his responsibility for the sheep. The crowds that again clustered around were "like sheep who had no shepherd." And so Jesus again began to talk with them, and to share with them the wholeness of God's love and acceptance that would make them complete. His teaching was of their worth in God's sight and that the power of worth gave them strength to live. Jesus gave of himself, still. Sometimes the rhythm of life is interrupted. The desired and necessary rest is once again pushed aside in order that the task of caring take place. That is the message of verses 30-34.

The lectionary text for this day jumps over two major events in Jesus' ministry, as recorded in Mark's sixth chapter. Next is the little boy's gift of five loaves and two fish that feed the multitude (Mark 6:35-44) and then is the story of Jesus' solitude in prayer that ended with his meeting the disciples, "walking on the sea." (Mark 6:45-52) These two texts are proposed for later study, so that today's scripture reading concludes with the general word about the crowds coming to Jesus for healing. Their faith was so strong that some begged "to be allowed to touch even the tassel of his robe; and all who touched it were restored to health." Those are Mark's words. Such was the faith in God's power through Jesus that even to touch the little prayer shawl tassel would bring healing.

We do not need to understand, with our scientific mind set, all the ways by which healing took place 2,000 years ago. If a broken life is made whole, it is a miracle whether it followed the science of psychology and medicine or was by an act of interrupting all the laws of nature! Blindness can be caused by acid thrown upon the eyes or by shellshock upon the mind. But the curing of blindness, no matter what the cause, is a miracle — then and now! The crippled limp is caused by the accidental crushing of bones or by some deep psychic trauma. But the curing of a crippled leg is a miracle — then and now. A body declared dead, whether from a heart stopped or a fevered coma, and then restored to life is miracle enough for any age. A life rejected and scorned and spit upon and told "you ain't worth nothing," is brought to wholeness with word of divine forgiveness and acceptance. That is a miracle whether on the Galilee shoreline or in the suburbs!

You see, we are that crowd that ran around the edge of the sea. We still come to Jesus for healing. We want only to reach out to him in spirit-touch. We still seek him that we might be forgiven for the sins we have done. In that forgiveness we can be healed. We seek him to confess the evil we have condoned. That confession, too, brings healing. We desire that the emotional burden we bear might be lifted from us — or shared. To share such a burden with Christ is to find healing. And, in his companionship, we can discover a wholeness that replaces the brokenness that is part of our life. Such discovery brings healing! His word upon the shoreline is the same word he speaks today. And the result is the same, for we, too, so often live as sheep without a shepherd!

We would see Jesus! We would look upon
The light in that divinely human face,
Where lofty majesty and tender grace
In blended beauty shone.

We would see Jesus, and would hear again
The voice that charmed the thousands by the sea,
Spoke peace to sinners, set the captives free,
And eased the sufferers' pain.

We would see Jesus, yet not him alone —
But see ourselves as in our Maker's plan;
And in the beauty of the Son of Man
See man upon his throne.

We would see Jesus, and let him impart
The truth he came among us to reveal,
Till in the gracious message we should feel
The beating of God's heart. Amen.

— W. J. Suckow

Lectionary Preaching
After Pentecost

Virtually all pastors who make use of the sermons in this book will find their worship life and planning shaped by one of two lectionary series. Most mainline Protestant denominations, along with clergy of the Roman Catholic Church, have now approved — either for provisional or official use — the three-year Common (Consensus) Lectionary. This family of denominations includes United Methodist, Presbyterian, United Church of Christ and Disciples of Christ.

Lutherans and Roman Catholics, while testing the Common Lectionary on a limited basis at present, follow their own three-year cycle of texts. While there are divergences between the Common and Lutheran/Roman Catholic systems, the gospel texts show striking parallels, with few text selections evidencing significant differences. Nearly all the gospel texts included in this book will, therefore, be applicable to worship and preaching planning for clergy following either lectionary.

A significant divergence does occur, however, in the method by which specific gospel texts are assigned to specific calendar days. The Common and Roman Catholic Lectionaries accomplish this by counting backwards from Christ the King (Last Sunday after Pentecost), discarding "extra" texts from the front of the list: Lutherans follow the opposite pattern, counting forward from The Holy Trinity, discarding "extra" texts at the end of the list.

The following index will aid the user of this book in matching the correct text to the correct Sunday during the Pentecost portion of the church year.

(Fixed dates do not pertain to Lutheran Lectionary)

Fixed Date Lectionaries *Common and Roman Catholic*	Lutheran Lectionary *Lutheran*
The Day of Pentecost	The Day of Pentecost
The Holy Trinity	The Holy Trinity
May 29-June 4 — Proper 4, Ordinary Time 9	Pentecost 2
June 5-11 — Proper 5, Ordinary Time 10	Pentecost 3
June 12-18 — Proper 6, Ordinary Time 11	Pentecost 4
June 19-25 — Proper 7, Ordinary Time 12	Pentecost 5
June 26-July 2 — Proper 8, Ordinary Time 13	Pentecost 6

July 3-9 — Proper 9, Ordinary Time 14	Pentecost 7
July 10-16 — Proper 10, Ordinary Time 15	Pentecost 8
July 17-23 — Proper 11, Ordinary Time 16	Pentecost 9
July 24-30 — Proper 12, Ordinary Time 17	Pentecost 10
July 31-Aug. 6 — Proper 13, Ordinary Time 18	Pentecost 11
Aug. 7-13 — Proper 14, Ordinary Time 19	Pentecost 12
Aug. 14-20 — Proper 15, Ordinary Time 20	Pentecost 13
Aug. 21-27 — Proper 16, Ordinary Time 21	Pentecost 14
Aug. 28-Sept. 3 — Proper 17, Ordinary Time 22	Pentecost 15
Sept. 4-10 — Proper 18, Ordinary Time 23	Pentecost 16
Sept. 11-17 — Proper 19, Ordinary Time 24	Pentecost 17
Sept. 18-24 — Proper 20, Ordinary Time 25	Pentecost 18
Sept. 25-Oct. 1 — Proper 21, Ordinary Time 26	Pentecost 19
Oct. 2-8 — Proper 22, Ordinary Time 27	Pentecost 20
Oct. 9-15 — Proper 23, Ordinary Time 28	Pentecost 21
Oct. 16-22 — Proper 24, Ordinary Time 29	Pentecost 22
Oct. 23-29 — Proper 25, Ordinary Time 30	Pentecost 23
Oct. 30-Nov. 5 — Proper 26, Ordinary Time 31	Pentecost 24
Nov. 6-12 — Proper 27, Ordinary Time 32	Pentecost 25
Nov. 13-19 — Proper 28, Ordinary Time 33	Pentecost 26 Pentecost 27
Nov. 20-26 — Christ the King	Christ the King

Reformation Day (or last Sunday in October) is October 31 (Common, Lutheran)

All Saints' Day (or first Sunday in November) is November 1 (Common, Lutheran, Roman Catholic)

Books In This Cycle B Series

Gospel Set

Christmas Is A Quantum Leap
Sermons For Advent, Christmas And Epiphany
Glenn Schoonover

From Dusk To Dawn
Sermons For Lent And Easter
C. Michael Mills

The Spirit's Tether
Sermons For Pentecost (First Third)
Leonard H. Budd

Assayings: Theological Faith Testings
Sermons For Pentecost (Middle Third)
Robert L. Salzgeber

Spectators Or Sentinels?
Sermons For Pentecost (Last Third)
Arthur H. Kolsti

First Lesson Set

Why Don't You Send Somebody?
Sermons For Advent, Christmas And Epiphany
Frederick C. Edwards

The Power To Change
Sermons For Lent And Easter
Durwood L. Buchheim

The Way Of The King
Sermons For Pentecost (First Third)
Charles Curley

The Beginning Of Wisdom
Sermons For Pentecost (Middle Third)
Sue Anne Steffey Morrow

Daring To Hope
Sermons For Pentecost (Last Third)
John P. Rossing